BEGINNINGS OF VIJAYANAGARA HISTORY

BEGINNINGS OF VIJAYANAGARA HISTORY

REV. H. HERAS, S. J.

GYAN

Published by

Gyan Publishing House
5, Ansari Road
Daryaganj, New Delhi-110002
Phone: 011-47034999, 9811692060
E-mail: books@gyanbooks.com

Distribution Network
gyanbooks.com
India, USA, Canada, UK, Australia

ISBN: 978-93-7169-463-6 (PB)

First Published, 1929

2nd Impression 2025

Printed at: Gyan Press, Delhi.

BEGINNINGS OF VIJAYANAGARA HISTORY
Author: REV. H. HERAS, S. J.

Beginnings of Vijayanagara History

Beginnings of Vijayanagara History

BY THE

REV. H. HERAS, S. J., M. A.

Professor of Indian History,
Director, Indian Historical Research Institute,
St Xavier's College, Bombay

1929

PREFACE

Two lectures delivered at the University of Mysore during the Dassera Holidays of 1928 form the subject of this book. It is a great pleasure to me to be able to make public my thankfulness to the University of Mysore for the kind invitation to deliver two extension lectures.

The subject selected for these lectures was first studied by Sewell, and then by H. Krishna Sastri and Dr. S. Krishnaswami Aiyangar. Anyhow the wish of affording my humble contribution to the history of the beginnings of that great Empire encouraged me to commence this study. I am only partly responsible for making it public; my friends and some of those who heard my lectures are also responsible with me.

Mr. George M. Moraes, M. A., one of my post graduate research students, has carefully prepared the Index.

The readers will, I hope, be sympathetic with us and will not exaggerate our guilt.

H. HERAS, S.J.

Bombay, June 24th, 1929.

CONTENTS

PART I

The Foundation of the City of Vijayanagara

1. Legendary Stories about the same. 1
2. Vidyāraṇya Śripada and the Foundation of Vijayanagara 11
3. The Origin of the Story of Vidyāraṇya. . . . 19
4. The Foundation of Vijayanagara according to Nuniz. 35
5. Critical Study of Ferishta's Account 42
6. The First Kings of Vijayanagara in Nuniz's Chronicle and Ballāḷa III . . . 45
7. The Foundation of Vijayanagara and the Defence of the Hoysaḷa Empire . . 48
8. The Ancient Names of the City of Vijayanagara . . 50
9. Vijayanagara called Hosapaṭṭaṇa 56

PART II

The Origin of the Sangama Dynasty

1. The Supporters of the Telugu Origin 61
2. The Enthronement of Harihara I by Vīra Ballāḷa III of the Hoysaḷa-Vaṁśa. . 65
3. Who was Saṅgama, the Father of Harihara. . . 69
4. The Ancestors of Saṅgama 74

5. Relationship between the Hoysaḷas and the First Vijayanagara Dynasty. . 78
6. The Brothers of Harihara I 93
7. The Hoysaḷa Country and the First Vijayanagara Rulers 102
8. Loyalty of the Vijayanagara Rulers to the Hoysaḷa Emperors. 109
9. The First Vijayanagara Emperors and the Telugu Country 118
Conclusion 123
Index. 133

PART I

The Foundation of the City of Vijayanagara

1. LEGENDARY STORIES ABOUT THE SAME

The Portuguese chronicler Nuniz after having narrated the enthronement of King Deorao in the city of Nagumdym, (Ānegondi), continues as follows:

"The King going one day a-hunting, as was often his wont, to a mountain on the other side of the river of Nagumdym, where now is the city of Bisnaga—which at that time was a desert place in which much hunting took place, and which the King had reserved for his own amusement—being in it with his dogs and appurtenances of the chase, a hare rose up before him, which instead of fleeing from the dogs, ran towards them and bit them all, so that none of them dared go near it for the harm that it did them. And seeing this, the King, astonished at so feeble a thing biting dogs which had already caught for him a tiger and a lion, judged it to be not really a hare but more likely some prodigy; and he at once turned back to the city of Nagumdym. And arriving at the river, he met a hermit who was walking along the bank, a man holy among them, to whom he told what had happened concerning the hare. And the hermit wondering at it, said to the King that he should turn back with him and show him the place where so marvellous a thing had happened; and being there, the hermit said that the King ought in that place to erect houses in which he could dwell, and build a city, for the prodigy meant that this would be the strongest city in the world, and that it would never be captured by his enemies, and would be the chief city in the kingdom. And so the King did, and on that very day began work on his houses, and he enclosed the city round about; and that done he left Nagumdym and soon filled the new city with people"[1].

This story narrated by Nuniz after the ancient chronicle which he is supposed to translate, is also repeated with some slight differences in two inscriptions, one in the Kolar District, and another in the Nellore District. The former runs as follows:—

"He (Harihara) ruled in Kuñjarakōṇa-puri (Ānegondi). On one occasion he crossed the Tuṅgabhadrā with the intention of hunting, and coming forth with his army, saw the forest to the south. And in the forest, that moon to the ocean Saṅgamēśa was surprised to see a fierce dog with long teeth, only chewing what had been bitten, and a hare. And seeing the god Virūpāksha along with the goddess Pampā, he did obeisance to them; and drawing near, paid respect to Vidyāraṇya, the yati in that temple, and informed him of the above very curious circumstance. The yatīndra, acquainted with the three times, smiled and said:—'O king this place is worthy to be the residence of a family of great kings; this is a specially strong site. Make here a city named Vidyā, equal to Alaka (Kubēra's city) with nine gates, wherein you may reside, like Purandara, in wealth acquired by victory in war on all sides, and hold the world in your serpent-like

[1] Sewell, *A Forgotten Empire*, p. 299-300. The style of this translation made by Mr. Sewell seems to be faulty. Yet we preferred to give the quotation as found in his classical pioneer history.

arms'. Thereupon Hariharēśvara, doing according to his direction, was seated on the throne"[1].

The account of the Nellore inscription reads as follows:—

"Once through desire of hunting, having crossed the Tuṅgabhadrā with his army, having reached its bank, the king Harihara saw a forest the south of it. Having beheld in that forest a certain hare engaged in copulation, which was fierce and was biting a dog and the female hare, the lord of man (the king) wondered. Having perceived this (hare) to be Śrī Virūpākshdēva associated with Pampādēvī, and humble with devotion, king Harihara, went to the hermit Vidyāraṇya, the incarnation of spiritual knowledge, whose austerity was honoured, and who was like another glorious Mahāṣēna (Śiva), near his temple. Having saluted in his vicinity with reverence (Vidyāranya) who was the store-house of austerity, and the receptacle of knowledge and arts, and who was very praiseworthy, he related this incident, whose explanation was wonderful. Having smiled a little, (Vidyāranya), the store-house of knowledge of the three times, the best of ascetics, said to that hero: 'Oh king, this country deserves to be the residence of a family of great kings, and the sole source of great power. Oh Lord, found a city named Vidyā, as beautiful as Alaka (Kubēra's city), which shall be a forest of learning (Irā-Sārasvatī, learning); and having reached the city having nine gates, and endowed with the glory of Indra, you bear the whole earth on your arm, which resembles the lord of serpents (Sēsha) and which has attained the state of the pleasure-grove of the Śrī of war who has been captured in battles. He thus instructed the king"[2].

These three versions of the legend of Harihara's hunting, so intimately connected with the foundation of Vijayanagara,

---

[1] *Ep. Carn.*, X, Bg, 70.

[2] Butterworth, *Inscriptions of the Nellore District*, I, p. 114-115.

not only do not agree with each other, but even the second and third account contradict some of the statements of the first. For instance, Nuniz says that the south side of the river Tuṅgabhadrā "was a desert place"; while the other two accounts speak of the temple of Virūpāksha as being already built on the same spot. These discrepancies and contradictions make them thoroughly untrustworthy. Nevertheless the two inscriptions bear a very early date, *viz.* 1336 and 1336-7, and that makes them contemporary with Harihara. Anyhow as regards the Kolar inscription Mr. Rice, the editor, says in a foot-note: "From its date this inscription would be of special interest, if authentic, but it cannot be depended on, being printed from a hand-copy supplied by the people, no original being forthcoming" [1]. And Mr. Butterworth, the editor of the Nellore inscription, likewise says as follows:—"The character is Naṇḍināgari but the formation of the letters is quite modern and in certain letters it is very similar to Dēvanāgari. This fact shows that the document is a fabrication"[2].

Both the documents, then, seem to be a fabrication. Now the date of this fabrication is to be ascertained; for if the fabrication is very early and almost contemporary with the event, the account is not to be rejected altogether. The internal comparative study of the text of the three accounts will disclose the date of the fabrication. The accounts will in future be named after the first letters of their place of origin in the two latter cases, and in the first case after the name of its author.

1 *Ep. Carn.*, X, p. 241, note 1.

2 Butterworth o. c., I, p. 109.

ACCOUNT Nu.	ACCOUNT K.	ACCOUNT Ne.
The King going one day a-hunting, as was often his wont, to a mountain on the other side of the river of Nagumdym, where now is the city of Bisnaga [1].	On one occasion he crossed the Tuṅgabhadrā with the intention of hunting, and coming forth with his army, saw the forests to the south.	Once through desire of hunting, having crossed the Tuṅgabhadrā with his army, having reached its bank, the king saw a forest to the south of it.
Being in it with his dogs and appurtenances of the chase, a hare rose up before him, which, instead of fleeing from the dogs, ran towards them and bit them all, so that none of them dared go near it for the harm that it did them.	And in the forest, that moon to the ocean Sangamēśa was surprised to see a fierce dog with long teeth only chewing what had been bitten, and a hare.	Having beheld in that forest a certain hare engaged in copulation, which was fierce and was biting a dog and the female hare, the lord of men wondered.
And seeing this, the King, astonished at so feeble a thing biting dogs	And seeing the god Virūpāksha along with the goddess Pampā,	Having perceived this (hare) to be Śrī Virūpākshadēva associat-

[1] The following parenthesis in the account of Nuniz evidently does not belong to the original chronicle translated by him. It is an explanation added by Nuniz himself.

ACCOUNT **Nu.**	ACCOUNT **K.**	ACCOUNT **Ne.**
which had already caught for him a tiger and a lion, judged it to be not really a hare but (more likely) some prodigy.	he did obeisance to them.	ed with Pampādēvi.
And he at once turned back to the city of Nagumdym. And arriving at the river, he met a hermit who was walking along the bank, a man holy among them, to whom he told what had happened concerning the hare.	And drawing near, paid respect to Vidyāraṇya, the yati in that temple, and informed him of the above very curious circumstance.	And humble with devotion King Harihara went to the hermit Vidyāraṇya, the incarnation of spiritual knowledge, whose austerity was honoured and who was like another glorious Mahāṣēna, near his temple. Having saluted in his vicinity with reverence (Vidyāraṇya), who was the store-house of austerity, and the receptacle of knowledge and arts, and who was very praiseworthy, he related this incident, whose explanation was very wonderful.

ACCOUNT Nu.

And the hermit, wondering at it, said to the King that he should turn back with him and show him the place where so marvellous a thing had happened; and being there, the hermit said that the King ought in that place to erect houses in which he could dwell, and build a city; for the prodigy meant that this would be the strongest city in the world, and that it would never be captured by his enemies and would be the chief city in the kingdom.

ACCOUNT K.

The yatīndra, acquainted with the three times, smiled and said;—'O king, this place is worthy to be the residence of a family of great kings; this is a specially strong site. Make here a city named Vidyā, equal to Alaka, with nine gates, wherein you may reside, like Purandara, in wealth acquired by victory in war on all sides, and hold the world in your serpent-like arms'.

ACCOUNT Ne.

Having smiled a little, (Vidyāraṇya) the storehouse of knowledge of the three times, the best of ascetics, said to that hero: — 'O king, this country deserves to be the residence of a family of great kings and the sole source of great power. Oh Lord, found a city named Vidyā, as beautiful as Alaka, which shall be a forest of learning; and having reached the city having nine gates, and endowed with the glory of Indra, you bear the whole earth on your arm, which resembles the lord of serpents and which has attained the state of the pleasure-grove of the Śrī of war who has been captured in battles'. He thus instructed the king.

From the inspection of the above table the following conclusions may be easily drawn:—

1. Accounts **K** and **Ne** are more similar to each other, and account **Nu** goes alone.

2. Account **Nu,** though sometimes more wordy, is nevertheless more sober than the other two.

3. The story of the hare as found in account **Nu** seems, on account of its simplicity, to be in its original state.

4. Accounts **K** and **Ne,** by adding new circumstances to the story of the hare, create some confusion.

5. The mythology added in accounts **K** and **Ne** suggests a later period.

6. Account **Nu** does not give the name of the ascetic, while accounts **K** and **Ne** not only give his name but also, specially account **Ne,** praise him to the skies.

7. The simplicity of the advice given Harihara by the ascetic in account **Nu** is absolutely distorted in accounts **K** and **Ne,** and specially in account **Ne,** on account of the adulation of Harihara and his family.

8. All these differences prove beyond doubt that account **Nu** is the oldest of the three; that accounts **K** and **Ne** were written in or about the same time, by persons who knew account **Nu** or a similar one, unknown to us; and that account **Ne** seems to be the most recent of the three.

Now the chronicle translated by Nuniz seems to have been written in the first half of the XVIth century, during the reign of Kṛishṇa Dēva Rāya; for it contains the narrative of part of that reign. Hence it is evident that accounts **K** and **Ne** were written somewhat afterwards, perhaps during the reign of Achyuta Dēva Rāya or Sadāśiva Rāya. Consequently the three accounts have no authority at all, and are to be rejected by impartial history.

The story of the hare is also related in a manuscript work entitled *Rājakālanirṇaya*. But this work seems to be of no historical value at all [1]. Quite to the point Mr. Sewell remarks as follows: "This same tale is told of many kings and chiefs in Southern India" [2]. One instance only will illustrate this statement of Mr. Sewell and will show once more how groundless is this narrative of the foundation of Vijayanagara.

The instance is found in the *Tazkarat-ul-Mulūk*, when it relates the foundation of the city of Bidar by Sultan Ahmad Shah Bahmāni: "One day when he went out hunting in the neighbourhood of Muhammadabad, a dog seized a hare by the tail. The hare turned round and fighting with the dog, overcame him. Sultan Ahmad on seeing this said:—'The climate of this country seems to be conducive to bravery, seeing that a hare beats a dog. If I should found a city here and make it my capital, the men who shall be born here and grow and thrive in the climate of this region will certainly be braver and more manly'" [3].

A similar story is related of one of the Nāyaks of Tarikere, before the foundation of this fort [4].

Other legendary stories are still related of the origin of the city of Vijayanagara. One says for instance that Bukka was a shepherd who had often waited on the ascetic Vidyāraṇya and supported him in his devotions. He was splendidly rewarded by the latter giving him a kingdom when the

Cf. Gopinatha Rao, *Srisailam Plates of Virupaksha*, *Ep. Ind.*, XV, p. 10.

Sewell, o. c., p. 299, note 1.

King, *History of the Bahmani Dynasty*, *Ind. An.*, XXVIII, p. 218.

Cf. Rice, *Mysore*, II, p. 447. (Bangalore, 1877).

royal line of the kings of Hampi became extinct[1]. Yet the story is not found in any authoritative document. Moreover the memory of Harihara, the first ruler of the new city, is here totally overlooked. The shepherd origin of many dynasties of south India is a fiction too well known to be believed any longer. Thus Ananda Kōn, a shepherd, accidentally found a treasure in a cave. With this money he made himself the head of a small band of warriors, and founded a small kingdom, that became afterwards the kingdom of Jinji[2].

Another of these stories states likewise that the ascetic Mādhava, through the favour of Bhuvanēśwarī, discovered a treasure with which he built the city of Vidyānagar or Vijayanagara, over which he reigned, and at the time of his death he left it to a Kuruba family[3]. According to this tradition, not recorded in any reliable document either, Vidyāraṇya would be the first ruler of Vijayanagara, a fact not supported by any contemporary authority. Such story is also related of other southern Indian dynasties. The above mentioned story of Ananda Kōn offers an example. Thus also the *Kēladi Arāsu Vamśāvali* refers that when one Chauda, a husbandman, was ploughing his land, his ploughshare struck considerable buried treasure. With it he managed to become the headman of the village, and as such he collected a small company of soldiers. He thus became the founder of the dynasty of the Ikeri Nāyaks[4]. Again Ferishta says the following about the founder of the Bahmāni Dynasty of Gulbar-

---

[1] Wilson, *The Mackenzie Collection* p. 83; Subramiah Pantulu, *Discursive Remarks on the Augustan Age of Telugu Literature*, *Int. Ant.*, XXVII, p. 247; Suryanarain Row, *The Never To Be Forgotten Empire*, p. 25.

[2] Cf. Srinivasachari, *The History of Gingee*, p. 5.

[3] Wilson, o. c., p. 83.

[4] Ibid., p. 333.

ga: "Hassan, a native of Delhi, was the servant of Jangu, a Brahmanical astrologer, enjoying high favour with Prince Muhammad Tuglak, and who in consideration of the good conduct of Hassan, gave him a pair of oxen, and permitted him to till a small piece of land for his own use. While at work one day, the plough attached itself to some substance, which on examination Hassan found to be a chain fastened to a copper vessel, containing a number of antique gold coins. On making the discovery, he carried the treasure to his master, who, commending him for his honesty, acquainted Prince Muhammad with the circumstance, who communicated it to his father the King. The monarch ordered Hassar to the presence, and conferred on him the command of one hundred horse" [1].

Hence we may finally say with Mr. Suryanarain Row: "There does not seem to be a single historical fact, which may be considered as certain in all these traditions and on which a reasonable argument may be based without fear of contradiction. Dates are contradictory and the details confusing" [2].

2. VIDYARANYA SRIPADA AND THE FOUNDATION OF VIJAYANAGARA.

There is still another story connected with the foundation of Vijayanagara that is to be critically examined before being admitted as historical. This is the story of the foundation cf the city by Mādhava, called also Vidyāraṇya Śrīpāda, the brother of the commentator Sayanna.

An inscription of the year (?) 1154 refers to this event when saying: "Having established a great ruler in Vidyānagara, prosperous is Vidyāraṇya-munīśvara" [3]. This inscript-

---

[1] Ferishta-Briggs, II, p. 284-285.
[2] Suryanarain Row, o. c., p. 27, note*.
[3] *Ep. Carn.*, VIII, Sh, 79.

ion nevertheless, on account of the date and other circumstances, seems to be spurious. There is another inscription of the year 1652 in the Śringeri Jagir, which is a little more explicit: "Formerly the guru of our line, author of the Vēda-bhāshya-Vidyāraṇya-śrīpāda, out of charity to the world, through the boon obtained by virtue of his penance from Virūpāksha dwelling on the banks of the Pampā, having founded Vidyānagara, for the protection of cows, gods and Brahmans performed the coronation anointing of Harihara-mahārāya to the throne" [1]. An inscription of 1538, of the time of Achyuta Dēva Rāya, speaks of "the throne of Vidyānagari, which Harihara Rāya had built and set up in the name of Vidyāranya-śrīpāda" [2]. Another inscription of King Sadāśiva, dated 1559, calls this monarch "Master of the throne of Vidyānagari, which Harihara Rāya caused to be built in the name of Vidyāraṇya" [3]. In another of the same monarch dated the year of the battle of Talikota we again find a reference to "Vipyānagari which Harihara-mahārāya built and consecrated in the name of Vidyāraṇya-śrīpāda" [4]. Finally the palm-leaf copy of a copper plate of the time of Śivappa Nāyaka of Ikeri (1652) informs us that Harihara I placed at the disposal of Vidyāraṇya 100 wṛiṭṭis of land forming Vidyāraṇyapura [5].

The story is slightly referred to, or sometimes presupposed, in many other inscriptions, specially of the XVIth century, and also in the chronicle of Nuniz [6]. Mr. B. Suryanarain Row mentions an "inscription found in one of the

Ep. Carn., VI, Sg, 11.
Ep. Carn., XI, Cd, 45.
Ibid., Cl, 54.
Ep. Carn., VII, Ci, 62.
M. A. R., 1925, p. 47.
Sewell, o. c., p. 300.

temples at Hampi left by the sage Vidyāraṇya"[1]. This inscription quoted by the author runs as follows: "On Wednesday, the 7th lunar day of the bright half of Visakha, in the year Dhatu, Sālivahana Śaka 1258, in an auspicious time with Guru (Jupiter) in the rising sign (Lagna), I, the prince of ascetics, have constructed this city in Vijayanagara"[2]. If this inscription is genuine, no doubt about the intervention of Vidyāraṇya in the foundation of Vijayanagara seems to be possible; but its authenticity is very doubtful; for the record is not to be found in any of the collections of inscriptions of Southern India, and the description of the document and the place where it is found is very vague and indefinite in the book of Mr. Suryanarain Row, who seems to publish it for the first time[3].

[1] Suryanarain Row, *The Never To Be Forgotten Empire*, p. 9.

[2] Ibid., p. 10.

[3] I made inquiries about this inscription at the office of the Government Epigraphist for India. The following is the reply I received:—

D. O. No. 117-1 / 1439-1313.
Government Epigraphist for India.
Ootacamund.
Dated the 6th October, 1928.

Dear Sir,

Please refer to your letter dated the 1st September 1928. The inscription you mention therein does not seem to have ever been copied by our department and is not represented in the Madras Epigraphical Collection. I have not seen a facsimile of it published anywhere and do not know if it is in existence at all.

Yours sincerely,
(Sgd.) *Hirananda Sastri.*

To

Rev. H. Heras, S. J.,
St. Xavier's College,
Cruickshank Road,
Fort—Bombay, 1.

In any case the difficulties arising against this connection of Vidyāraṇya with the foundation of Vijayaṇagara are historical rather than epigraphical or palaeographical. From not having considered these difficulties several authors have taken for granted the historicity of this story, as Sewell [1], Krishnaswami Aiyangar [2], Krishnamacharlu, [3], Krishna Sastri [4], Suryanarain Row [5], etc. In one of my previous papers, I also referred to Vidyāraṇya as the great helper of Harihara in the foundation of Vijayanagara [6]. I now acknowledge my mistake.

The objections against this story are the following:—

1. Prescinding from the inscription published by Mr. Suryanarain Row, the authenticity of which is very doubtful, there is no contemporary epigraphical record stating the participation of Vidyāraṇya in the foundation of Vijayanagara. The earliest inscriptions mentioning this fact seem to be dated during the third dynasty.

2. Mādhava, called also Vidyāraṇya, according to an inscription of 1347, was the minister of Mārapa, the fourth brother of Harihara I, at Chandragutti, the capital of the Banavasi Twelve-thousand [7]. Had he been the founder of the city of Vijayanagara and rendered such great help to Harihara in settling the affairs of the kingdom (as the tradit-

---

1 Sewell, I, p. 106.

2 S. Krishnaswamy Aiyangar, *Some Contributions of South India to Indian Culture*, p. 309.

3 Krishnamacharlu, *The Religion of the Vijayanagara House, Ind. Ant.*, XLIV, p. 219-221.

4 Krishna Sastri, *The First Vijayanagara Dynasty*, A.S. of I, Report, 1907-8, p. 239.

5 Suryanarain Row, o. c., p. 9-10.

6 Heras, *Goa Viragal of the Time of Harihara II*, *Q. J. M. S.*, XIX, p. 23.

7 *Ep. Carn.*, VIII, Sb, 375.

ion seems to suppose), one can hardly believe that Harihara should have parted with him in order that he should become the minister of his brother.

3. The tradition supposes that Mādhavāchārya was at the time of the foundation of Vijayanagara, not only an ascetic, but the guru or head of the Śaiva math at Śringeri. Yet, in the year 1346 Harihara I with his four brothers, his son-in-law and others paid a visit to the Śringeri math, and made a grant to Bhāratī-tīrtha-śrīpāda, and his disciples[1]. Now this Bhāratī-tīrtha-śrīpāda, also called Bhāratī Krishṇa-tīrtha, is the immediate predecessor of Vidyāraṇya in the succession list of the Jagad-gurus of the Śringeri math[2]. Hence it is evident that at the time of the foundation of Vijayanagara, Vidyāraṇya was not the guru of Śringeri. Moreover the inscription does not mention Vidyāraṇya at all, a thing that would appear incredible, had he been the great benefactor of Harihara and his family.

4. In 1356 Bukka I visits Śringeri and makes a grant to Vidyātīrtha-Śrīpāda, but neither the stone inscriptions recording the fact, nor the Śringeri plates of Harihara II, that mention the same event, say a word of Vidyāraṇya or of his activities in Vijayanagara[3].

5. Sometime after 1356 Bukka I wrote a letter to Vidyāraṇya, who was then at Vārānasi (Benares), requesting him to return to Virūpāksha (Vijayanagara). Bukka enclosed in his letter an order of the senior Śrīpāda (Vydyātīrtha) to the same effect[4]. This order he gladly obeyed; as he had great reverence towards that guru[5].

---

1 *Ep. Carn.*, VI, Sg, 1.
2 Cf. Rice, *Mysore*, I, p. 380.
3 *M. A. R.*, 1916, p. 56 and 57.
4 Ibid., p. 57.
5 Cf. Narasimhachar, *Madhavacharya and his Younger Brothers*, *Ind. Ant.*, XLV, p. 3.

6. Some time after, Bukka pays another visit to Śringeri in company of Vidyāraṇya, to whom he makes a grant, without any reference to the supposed help rendered to his brother Harihara [1].

7. An inscription of the year 1368 speaks at length of the excellent qualities of Mādhava, who is called the minister of Bukka, and nothing is said about the foundation of Vijayanagara [2].

8. In the Śringeri copper-plates of Harihara II of the year 1380, "Vidyāraṇya's feats are stated to be more wonderful than those of Brahma seeing that he can make the eloquent dumb, and the dumb, the most eloquent". Similar things are said of Vidyātīrtha and of Bhāratītīrtha, but the foundation of Vijayanagara is not mentioned at all in order to extol Vidyāraṇya over the other two gurus [3].

9. In another set of copper-plates of Harihara II, of the year 1384, it is said that "by the grace of Vidyāraṇya-muni he (Harihara) acquired the empire of knowledge unattainable by other kings" [4]. This was the proper place to say that Harihara II acquired the empire of knowledge from Vidyāraṇya, just as Harihara I obtained from him the empire of the world. Yet nothing of the kind is said.

11. In 1386 Vidyāraṇya dies at Hampi (Vijayanagara) according to a *Kaḍita* at Śringeri [5]. No mention is made of Vijayanagara as founded by him.

12. In the same year Harihara II makes a grant of lands, under the name of Vidyāraṇya-pura, to the Śringeri math, to commemorate the death of Mādhava Vidyāraṇya [6]. The

---

[1] *M. A. R.*, 1916, p. 57.

[2] *Ep. Carn.*, VII, Sk, 281. Cf. Aufrecht, *Oxford Catalogue*, p. 264.

[3] *M. A. R.*, 1916, p. 56.

[4] Ibid., p. 58. [5] Ibid., p. 59. [6] Ibid.

foundation of Vijayanagara is also totally overlooked here.

13. Another unfinished inscription of Harihara II of the same date contains the following praises of the great guru: "May the wonderful glances of Vidyāraṇya, which resemble showers of camphor dust, garlands of the kalhāra flower, rays of the moon, sandal paste and waves of the milk ocean, and which shower the nectar of compassion, bring you happiness! Can he be Brahma? We do not see four faces. Can he be Vishnu? He has not got four arms. Can he be Śiva? No oddness of the eyes is observed. Having thus argued for a long time, the learned have come to the conclusion that Vidyāraṇya is the supreme light incarnate"[1]. Inspite of this great eulogy Vidyāraṇya's share in the foundation of Vijayanagara is passed over in silence.

14. Harihara II's son, Prince Chikka Rāya, who was ruling the kingdom of Āraga, had granted several lands to Vidyāranya, without mentioning any of his supposed achievements in Vijayanagara[2].

Hence it is clear that the contemporary inscriptions, which mention Vidyāraṇya, and could know of his participation in the early affairs of the Empire, and had splendid opportunities to narrate it, do not mention such participation at all. While the only documents that refer to this event are some very posterior inscriptions and chronicles, and some fabricated lithic records. After considering all this, it may be affirmed that the foundation of Vijayanagara by Mādhava Vidyāraṇya, and the abishēka ceremony of Harihara I performed by the same guru are wholly groundless fables. Mr. Gopinatha Rao had independently arrived at the same conclusion: "Again Vidyāraṇya, who rose to prominence only in the reign of Bukka

[1] *M. A. R.* 1916, p. 58.

[2] Ibid., p. 57.

and his son Harihara II, cannot be the person who advised Harihara I to construct the city of Vijayanagara" [1].

Hence the historical events of the life of Vidyāraṇya connected with the history of Vijayanagara are only the following:—

1346. Vidyāraṇya was not yet the Jagad-guru of the Śringeri math.

1347. Vidyāraṇya is the minister of Mārapa Voḍeyar in the kingdom of Banavasi Twelve-thousand.

1356. Vidyāraṇya was not yet the Jagad-guru of Śringeri.

1356. Vidyāraṇya, residing at Benares, is invited by Bukka I and ordered by Vidyātīrtha Śrīpāda to come back to Vijayanagara.

1368. Vidyāraṇya is said to be the minister of Bukka I. Another inscription calls him Mahāpradhāna (Prime Minister) and states that he is ruling the Banavasi Twelve-thousand, as a subordinate of Bukka I.

1380. Great eulogy of Vidyāraṇya in an inscription of Harihara II. He seems to be already the guru of Śringeri. (In fact his predecessor Bhāratī Krishṇa-tīrtha seems to have died that year) [2].

1384. Harihara II confesses to have acquired much knowledge from the teachings of Vidyāraṇya.

1385. By this time Prince Chikka Rāya, son of Harihara II and governor of the kingdom of Āraga, makes a grant of lands to Vidyāraṇya.

1386. Death of Vidyāraṇya at Hampi (Vijayanagara). Harihara II makes a grant of lands to the Śringeri math to commemorate his death. Another inscription of the same king contains a kind of funeral eulogy of the learned guru.

---

[1] Gopinatha Rao, *Srisailam Plates of Virupaksha*, *Ep. Ind.*, XV, p. 11.

[2] Cf. Rice, *Mysore*, I, p. 380.

3. THE ORIGIN OF THE STORY OF VIDYARANYA.

Before ending this subject it will be opportune to study the origin of this fable. This will not be difficult if we pay attention to the fact that this story of Vidyāraṇya is connected with the name Vidyānagara given some times to the capital of the Empire; in fact the name Vidyānagara supposes the veracity of the legend of Vidyāraṇya. In the following table the names given to the capital in different inscriptions will be found arranged in chronological order:—

Year of the inscription	King in whose reign inscription was issued	Name given to the capital	District where inscription is found	Reference
		Sangama Dynasty		
1336	Harihara I	Vidyānagara	Kolar	*EC*, X, Bg, 70.
1336-7	»	Kuñjarakōṇa	Nellore	*NI*, I, p. 114.
1347	»	Vijayanagar	Shimoga	*EC*, VIII, Sb, 375.
1347	»	Hastini	»	Ibid.
1354	Bukka I	Hosapaṭṭaṇa		*MAR*, 1295, p. 74.
1354	»	Vidyānagara	Tumkūr	*EC*, XII, Pg, 74.
1355	»	Hosapaṭṭaṇa	Chitaldroog	*EC*, XI, Cd, 2.
1366	»	Vijayanagara	Tumkūr	*EC*, XII, Pg, 18.
1368	»	Vijayanagara	Shimoga	*EC*, VII, Sk, 881.
1369	»	Hastināvati	Kadūr	*EC*, VI, Kp, 6.
1370	»	Vijanagara (*sic*)	Tumkūr	*EC*, XII, Mi, 74.
1370	»	City named Vidyā	Kolar	*EC*, X, Gd, 46.

Year of the inscription	King in whose reign inscription was issued	Name given to the capital	District where inscription is found	Reference
1377	Bukka I	Vijayanagara		*MAR*, 1914-15, p. 58.
1378	»	City of victory	Hassan	*EC*, V, Cn, 256.
1379	»	City named Vijaya	Chitaldroog	*EC*, XI, Dg, 34.
1379	»	City named Vijaya	Chitaldroog	Rice, *MI*, p. 55.
1379	Harihara II	Hastināvati	Shimoga	*EC*, VII, Hl, 84.
1379	»	City of Vijaya		Rice, *MI*, p. 55.
1379-80	»	City that bore the name of Vijaya		*JBBRAS*, XII, p. 373.
1379-80	»	Vijayanagara		Ibid., p. 376.
1380	»	Vijayanagari	Shimoga	*EC*, VIII, Sb, 152.
1382	»	Vijayanagara	Chitaldroog	*EC*, XI, Dg, 68.
1383	»	Vijayanagari	Hassan	*EC*, V, Bl, 75.
1384	»	Vijayanagari		*MAR*, 1916, p. 58.
1387	»	Vijayanagari	Hassan	*EC*, VIII, Sb, 512.
1388	»	Vijayanagari	Hassan	Ibid., 146.
1390	»	Vijayanagari	Shimoga	*EC*, VII, Hl, 6.
1392	»	Vidyānagara	Kadūr	*EC*, VI, Kp, 49.
1392	»	Vijayanagari	Tumkūr	*EC*, XII, Pg, 72.
1393	»	Vijayanagara	Shimoga	*EC*, VIII, Sb, 154.

Year of the inscription	King in whose reign inscription was issued	Name given to the capital	District where inscription is found	Reference
1394	Harihara II	Vijayanagari	Shimoga	*EC*, VII, Ci, 13.
1395	»	Hastinapura-Vijayanagara	»	*EC*, VIII, Sb, 103.
1395	»	Vijayanagari	Kolar	*EC*, X, Sp, 54.
1395	»	Vijayanagara	Tumkūr	*EC*, XII, Tp, 44.
1396	»	Vijayanagari	Shimoga	*EC*, VII, Hl, 71.
1396	»	Vijayanagari	Hassan	*EC*, V, HN, 7.
1396	»	Vijayanagari	Shimoga	*EC*, VIII, Tl, 8.
1397	»	Vijayanagari	Hassan	*EC*, V, Bl, 3.
1399	»	Vijayanagari	Shimoga	*EC*, VIII, Tl, 215.
1401	»	Vijayanagara	Tumkūr	*EC*, XII, Pg, 82.
1403	»	Vijayanagari	Shimoga	*EC*, VII, Hl, 68.
1403	»	Vijayānagari	Kadūr	*EC*, VI, Kp, 52.
1404	»	Vijayanagari	Shimoga	*EC*, VIII, Tl, 196.
1404	»	Vijayanagari	»	Ibid., 133.
1404	»	Vijayanagari	»	Ibid., 130.
1404	»	Vijayanagari	»	Ibid., 13.
1404	»	Vijayanagari	»	Ibid., 11.
1404	»	Vijayanagari	»	Ibid., 9.
1404	»	Vijayanagari	Hassan	*EC*, V, Ag, 52.
1404	»	Vijayanagara-Hastinati	Shimoga	*EC*, VII, Ci, 28.
?	»	Vidyānagari	Mysore	*MAR*, 1912-13, p. 42.
1404	Bukka II	Vijayanagari	Kadūr	*EC*, VI, Kp, 25.
1405	»	Vijayānagari	Shimoga	*EC*, VIII, Tl, 126.

Year of the inscription	King in whose reign inscription was issued	Name given to the capital	District where inscription is found	Reference
1405	Bukka II	Vijayanagari	Shimoga	Ibid., 22.
1405	»	Vijayanagari	»	Ibid., 12.
1406	»	The nagari named Vijaya	Hassan	*EC*, V, Hn, 133.
1407	Dēva Rāya I	Vijayanagari	Shimoga	*EC*, VIII, Tl, 190.
1407	»	Vijayanagari	»	Ibid., 122.
1408	»	Vijayanagari	»	Ibid., 222.
1408	»	Vijayanagara	»	Ibid., 131.
1408	»	Vijayanagar		*MAR*, 1925, p. 45.
1408	»	Vijayanagari	Kolar	*EC*, X, Mb, 175.
1409	»	Vijayanagari	Kadūr	*EC*, VI, Kp, 26.
1409	»	Vijayanagara	Shimoga	*EC*, VII, Sh, 70.
1410	»	Vijayanagara	Chitaldroog	*EC*, XI, Hr, 28.
1410	»	Vijayanagari	Shimoga	*EC*, VIII, Tl, 205.
1410	Vīra Vijaya	The city named Vijaya	Bangalore	*EC*, IX, Ht, 34.
1411	»	Vijayanagari	Shimoga	*EC*, VIII, Tl, 142.
1413	»	Anegondi		*MAR*, 1911-12, p. 49.
1413	»	[Vid]yānagara	Shimoga	*EC*, VII, Sh, 30.
1415	»	Vijayanagari	Shimoga	*EC*, VIII, Tl, 217.
1415	»	Vijayanagara	Tumkūr	*EC*, XII, Mi, 83.
1417	»	Vijayanagara	Tumkūr	Ibid., Pg, 96.

Year of the inscription	King in whose reign inscription was issued	Name given to the capital	District where inscription is found	Reference
1417	Vijaya Vīra	Vidyānagari	Shimoga	*EC*, VIII, Tl, 148.
1417	»	Vijayanagari	»	*EC*, VII, Sk, 37.
1420	»	Vijayanagari	»	*EC*, VIII, Tl, 168.
1420	»	Vidyānagari	»	*EC*, VII, Sk, 288.
1421	»	Vijayanagari	»	*EC*, VIII, Tl, 144.
1423	»	Vijayanagara	»	Ibid., 14.
1423	»	Vijayanagari	»	Ibid., 2.
1424	Dēva Rāya II	Vijayanagari	»	Ibid., 175.
1424	»	Vijayanagari	»	Ibid., 170.
1426	»	Vijayanagara	Tumkūr	*EC*, XII, Tm, 11.
1427	»	Vijayanagara	Kadūr	*EC*, VI, Kp, 27.
1430	»	The royal city whose name is Vijaya	Chitaldroog	*EC*, XI, Cd, 29.
1430	»	Vijayanagari	Shimoga	*EC*, VII, Sk, 40.
1431	»	Vijayanagara	»	*EC*, VIII, Tl, 1.
1431	»	Vijayanagari	»	Ibid., Sa, 51.
1431	»	Vijəyanagara	»	*EC*, VII, Sh, 71.
1431	»	Vijayanagara	Bangalore	*EC*, IX, Bn, 127.
1432	»	Vijayanagara		*MAR*, 1916, p. 60.
1432	»	Hampe-Hastināvati	Hassan	*EC*, V, Cn, 241.
1432	»	Vijayanagari	»	Ibid.
1434	»	Vijayanagari	Kolar	*EC*, X, Sd, 94.
1436	»	Hampe-Hastināvati	Shimoga	*EC*, VIII, Sb, 490.

Year of the inscription	King in whose reign inscription was issued	Name given to the capital	District where inscription is found	Reference
1436	Dēva Rāya II	Hastināvati		*MAR*, 1920, p. 36.
1441	»	Vidyānagara	Shimoga	Ibid., Sa, 68.
1442	»	Vijayanagar		*MAR*, 1913-14, p. 47.
1442	»	Vijayanagar	Chitaldroog	*EC*, XI, Hr, 14.
1442	»	Hastināvati	Shimoga	*EC*, VIII, Sb, 489.
1442	»	Vijayanagari	»	Ibid., 163.
1445	»	The city name Vijaya	»	Ibid., Tl, 200.
1445	»	Hastināvati	»	Ibid., Sb, 495.
1445	»	The city named Vijaya	Tumkūr	*EC*, XII, Tm, 37.
?	»	Vijanagara (*sic*)	Shimoga	*EC*, VIII, Nr, 29.
1448	Mallikārjuna	Vijayanagari	Kadūr	*EC*, VI, Kp, 32.
1448	»	Vijayanagari	Kadūr	*EC*, VI, Kp, 32.
1448	»	Vijayanagari	Shimoga	*EC*, VIII, Sb, 473.
1450	»	Vijayanagari	»	Ibid., Tl, 155.
1450	»	Vijaya the royal city	»	Ibid., Nr, 67.
1451	»	Vijayanagari	Kadūr	*EC*, VI, Kp, 44.
1454	»	Vijayanagari	Shimoga	*EC*, VIII, Sb, 167.
1455	»	Vijayanagara	»	*EC*, VIII, Nr, 65.
1460	»	Vijayanagari	»	Ibid., Sa, 2.

Year of the inscription	King in whose reign inscription was issued	Name given to the capital	District where inscription is found	Reference
1468	Virūpāksha	Vidyānagara	Shimoga	Ibid., Tl, 143.
1475	„	Vijayanagara	„	Ibid., Sb, 527.
1478	„	Hastināvati	Hassan	*EC*, V, Cn, 153.
		Saluva Dynasty		
1486	Narasiṁha	Vidyānagara	Tumkūr	*EC*, XII, Tm, 54.
		Tuluva Dynasty		
1505	Vīra Narasiṁha	Vidyānagari	Kolar	*EC*, X, Gd, 77.
1510	Kṛishṇa Dēva Rāya	Vijayanagara	Tumkūr	*EC*, XII, Tm, 43.
1510	„	Vidyānagara	Shimoga	*EC*, VII, Sk, 234.
1511	„	Vijayanagara	Chitaldroog	*EC*, XI, Hk, 94.
1512-3	„	Vijayanagara		*JBBRAS*, XII, p. 392.
1513	„	Vijayanagara	Shimoga	*EC*, VII, Sh, 1.
1514	„	Vijayanagar		*MAR*, 1920, p. 37.
1515	„	Vidyānagara	Kadūr	*EC*, VI, Mg, 88.
1515	„	Vijayanagara	Hassan	*EC*, V, Hn, 6.
1516	„	Vijayanagara	Kadūr	*EC*, VI, Mg, 41.
1520	„	Hampe Hastināvati	„	Ibid., 27.
1523	„	Vijayanagara		*MAR*, 1918, p. 52.
1524	„	Vijayanagara	Kadūr	*EC*, VI, Mg, 62.
1524	„	Hampe	Hassan	*EC*, V, Bl, 78.
1525	„	Vijayanagara	Tumkūr	*EC*, XII, Pg, 72.

Year of the inscription	King in whose reign inscription was issued	Name given to the capital	District where inscription is found	Reference
1525	Kṛishṇa Dēva Rāya	Vijayanagari		*MAR*, 1925, p. 23.
1525	»	Vijayanagara	Tumkūr	*EC*, XII, Tp, 10.
1527	»	Vidyānagara	Shimoga	*EC*, VIII, Sb, 527.
?	»	Anegondi		*MAR*, 1919, p. 35.
1530	Achyuta Dēva Rāya	Vidyānagara	Mysore	*EC*, III, Ml, 105.
1530	»	Vidyānagari	Hassan	*EC*, V, Cn, 187.
1531	»	Vidyānagara	Chitaldroog	*EC*, XI, Dg, 31.
1531	»	Vidyānagara	Hassan	*EC*, V, Hn, 1.
1532	»	Vidyānagara	Mysore	*MAR*, 1920, p. 37.
1532	»	Vidyānagari	Hassan	*EC*, V, Hn, 115.
1532	»	Vidyānagari	»	Ibid., 119.
1533	»	Vijayanagara	Chitaldroog	*EC*, XI, Hk, 132.
1535	»	Hampe-Hastināvati	Hassan	*EC*, V, Bl, 223.
1535	»	Vijayanagari	Tumkūr	*EC*, XII, Ck, 44.
1535	»	Vijayanagari	»	Ibid., 5.
1535	»	Vidyānagara	Mysore	*EC*, III, Ml, 34.
1537	»	Vidyanāgari	»	Ibid., 59
1538	»	Vidyānagari	Chitaldroog	*EC*, XI, Cd, 45
1539	»	Vidyānagarī	Tumkūr	*EC*, XII, Tm, 50.
1539	»	Hampe-Hastināvati	Kadūr	*EC*, VI, Cm, 80.
1539	»	Vijayanagara	Hassan	*EC*, V, Bl, 197.

Year of the inscription	King in whose reign inscription was issued	Name given to the capital	District where inscription is found	Reference
1540	Archyuta Dēva Rāya	Vidyānagara	Chitaldroog	*EC*, XI, Hk, 62.
1540	»	Vidyānagara	»	Ibid., 71.
1540	»	Vidyānagara	»	Ibid., 111.
1542	»	Vijayanagari	Kadūr	*EC*, VI, Mg, 64.
1544	Sadāśiva Rāya	Vidyānagara	Kolar	*MAR*, 1813-14, p. 49.
1546-7	»	Vidyānagar	Nellore	Butterworth, III, p. 1184.
1548	»	Hastināvati	Hassan	*EC*, V, Hn, 152.
1548	»	Hampe-Hastināvati	»	Ibid., Bl, 4.
1550	»	Vijayanagara	Tumkūr	*EC*, XII, Tp, 6.
1550	»	Vidyānagara	Shimoga	*EC*, VIII, Nr, 77.
1550	»	Hampe-Hastināvati	»	Ibid.
1551	»	Vidyānagara	Chitaldroog	*EC*, XI, Jl, 24.
1551	»	Vidyānagari	»	Ibid., Mk, 8.
1552	»	Vijayanagara		*MAR*, 1913-14, p. 48.
1552	»	Vidyānagari	Kadūr	*EC*, VI, Mg, 40.
1553	»	Vidyānagari in Hampe	»	Ibid., Kp, 17.
1554	»	Vidyānagari	Chitaldroog	*EC*, XI, Dg, 22.
1554	»	Vidyānagara	Hassan	Rice, *MI*, p. 225.
1554	»	Vidyānagara	Chitaldroog	*EC*, XI, Hr, 22.
1555	»	Vijayanagari	Tumkūr	*EC*, XII, Ck, 6.
1555	»	Vidyānagara	Hassan	*EC*, V, Bl, 5.
1556	»	Vidyānagara	Chitaldroog	*EC*, XI, Mk, 4.
1557	»	Vidyānagari	Shimoga	*EC*, VII, Hl, 9.

Year of the inscription	King in whose reign inscription was issued	Name given to the capital	District where inscription is found	Refereuce
1558	Sadāśiva Rāya	Vidyānagara	Tumkūr	*EC*, XII, Pg, 21.
1559	»	Vidyānagari	Chitaldroog	*EC*, XI, Cl, 54.
1560	»	Vijayanagar	Tumkūr	*EC*, XII, Tm, 4.
1560	»	Vidyānagari	Shimoga	*EC*, VIII, Tl, 103.
1561	»	Vidyānagara	Hassan	*EC*, V, Hn, 7.
1562	»	Hastināvati-Vidyānagari	»	Ibid., 15.
1562	»	Vidyānagara	Chitaldroog	*EC*, XI, Dg, 30.
1562	»	Vijayanagara	Tumkūr	*EC*, XII, Tm, 44.
1562	»	Vidyānagara	Chitaldroog	*EC*, XI, Dg, 83.
1563	»	Hastināvati-Vidyānagari	Hassan	*EC*, V, Hn, 2.
1566	»	Vidyānagara	Shimoga	*EC*, VIII, Sb, 357.
1566	»	Vidyānagari	»	Ibid., Nr, 1.
1568	»	Vidyānagari	Chitaldroog	*EC*, XI, Hl, 47.
		Aravidu Dynasty		
1571	Tirumala Rāya	Hastināvati	Tumkūr	*EC*, XII, Tm, 1.
1577	»	Vidyānagari	Shimoga	*EC*, VIII, Tl, 5.
1587	Veṅkaṭa II	Hampe-Hastināvati	Kadūr	*EC*, VI, Cm, 79.
1627	Rāma II	Vidyānagara	Tumkūr	*EC*, XII, Mi, 32.
1659	Raṅga III	Vidyānagara	Hassan	*EC*, V, Ag, 57.
1669	Veṅkata IV	Vijayanagara	Tumkūr	*EC*, XII, Ck, 38.

Among the 196 inscriptions examined for this purpose 31 inscriptions refer to the ancient name of the city, 111 give the name Vijayanagara and only 54 give the name Vidyānagara. But what is still more interesting is to note

(To face p. 29).

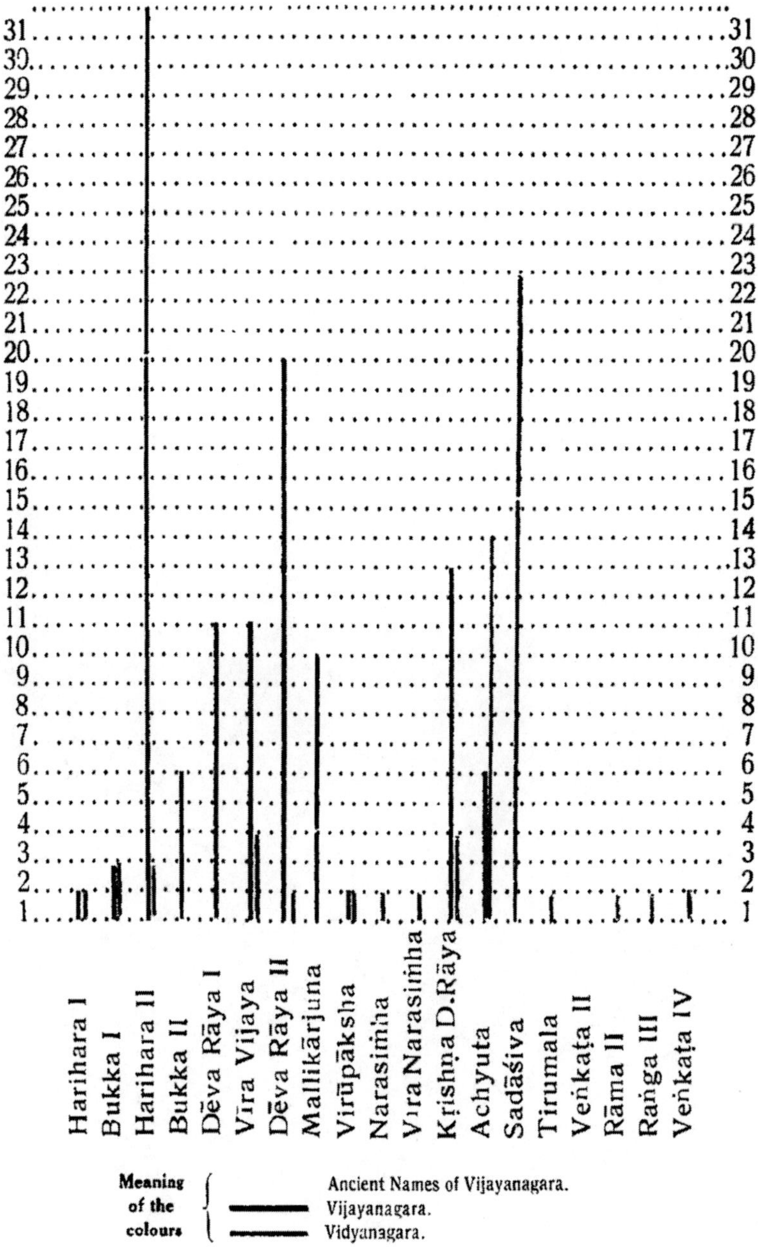
1 2 3 4 5 6 7 8 9 10 11 12 13 14 15 16 17 18 19 20 21 22 23 24 25 26 27 28 29 30 31
Harihara I
Bukka I
Harihara II
Bukka II
Dēva Rāya I
Vīra Vijaya
Dēva Rāya II
Mallikārjuna
Virūpāksha
Narasiṁha
Vīra Narasiṁha
Kṛishṇa D. Rāya
Achyuta
Sadāśiva
Tirumala
Veṅkaṭa II
Rāma II
Raṅga III
Veṅkaṭa IV
Meaning of the colours
Ancient Names of Vijayanagara.
Vijayanagara.
Vidyanagara.

the proportion existing between these two names in the reigns of the different sovereigns. This proportion will be seen in the accompanying graph.

After a careful examination of the preceding table, and adjoining graph, the following conclusions may be easily drawn:—

1. Contrary to all expectations the word Vidyānagara is very litte used and practically unknown during the first dynasty.

2. The few inscriptions examined of the second dynasty do not allow us to make any statement as regards this period.

3. In the beginning of the third dynasty, including the reign of Kṛishṇa Dēva Rāya, the word Vidyānagara is used more or less as during the first dynasty. Nevertheless the practice of using it increases during the reign of Achyuta Dēva Rāya and reaches its climax in the one of Sadāśiva Rāya.

4. Vidyānagara also seems to prevail during the fourth dynasty.

5. This striking increase in calling the capital of the Empire after the name of Vidyāraṇya naturally invites the researcher to carefully examine the few inscriptions which give the same name in the early years of Vijayanagara, and specially during the reigns of the monarchs of the Saṅgama family:—

Reign of Harihara I.

1336 Mr. Rice suspects that the inscription is not genuine [1].

Reign of Bukka I.

1354. The inscription also seems to be spurious, as it grants imperial titles to Bukka I, who never

---

[1] *Ep. Carn.*, X, p. 241.

assumed them. Moreover Bukka is said to be "seated on the jewel throne" one year before Harihara I's death.

1370. As noted by Mr. Rice, this inscription offers a great difficulty as regards the date: "This is given as the Śaka 1216, the year Tārana. But this does not fall within Bukka's reign, during which there was no Tārana"[1]. This is most likely due to a miscalculation of the one who composed the inscription. Such miscalculation cannot be conceived if the writer gives the date of the current year, while it is very easy in the case of a forger of past documents. Such seems to be the present case.

Reign of Harihara II.

1392. No remark to be made.

? Mr. Narasimhachar says the following about this inscription: "This grant is peculiar in several respects. It differs from all the published copper-plate inscriptions of Harihara not only in the arrangement of facts but also in giving the king's titles and genealogy and in the mode of giving the date. The genealogy is not supported by any inscription that we know of. The intended date is perhaps Śaka 1302 (A. D. 1379), but there was no solar eclipse in that year. There was an eclipse in Kārtika of Siddhārthi corresponding to A. D. 1319, but this year is too early for either Harihara of Vijayanagar dynasty. Further, the record is disfigured

---

[1] Ibid., p. 219.

by numerous grammatical and orthographical errors. These circumstances are sufficient to raise a reasonable doubt as to the genuineness of the grant"[1].

Reign of Vīra Vijaya.

1413. The date of the grant is doubtful. Moreover there are several gaps in the inscription, one of these occurring in the beginning of the word that speaks of the residence of the king; the last four syllables of the word are only readable, thus: yānagara. The editor has supplemented the letters missing and has made: (Vid)yāganara. The first long ā of the readable portion seems to have induced him to accept this reading. Yet there are some cases in the inscriptions in which Vijayanagara also appears with the second a long, thus: Vijayānagara. See for instance inscription of 1403 in the reign of Harihara II.

1417. No remark to be made.

1420. No remark to be made.

Reign of Dēva Rāya II.

1441. The date of the inscription is doubtful.

Reign of Virūpāksha.

1468. No remark to be made.

Reign of Narasiṁha.

1486. The date of the inscription is also doubtful.

6. The preceding observations have proved that out of 11 inscriptions of the first two dynasties that give the name Vidyānagara, only four inscriptions are not either evidently spurious or at least doubtful. And these four, after consider-

---

[1] *M.A.R.*, 1912-1913, p. 42.

ing all that has been said hitherto, are also to be declared not genuine.

7. Hence we agree with Mr. Burnell, when he states that Vijayanagara is the most ancient form [1], a fact which was also noted by Mr. Fleet: "In more modern descriptions", says he, "the name is written 'Vijayanagari', and is further corrupted into 'Vidyānagari' " [2]. And even in Bengali literature, the word Vidyānagara is only found in a later period [3].

8. All these facts point to a definite cause in the beginning of the third Dynasty that produced this corruption of the word, and connected it with the foundation of the city by Mādhava Vidyāranya. Such a corruption was not precisely a philological corruption of the word, but a deliberate and intended corruption, as the fact of the forgery of several grants connected with the story clearly discloses.

9. Where the forgery of all these grants was committed, and where the story of Vidyāranya as the founder of Vijayanagara arose, will be seen by studying the geographical position of the inscriptions that give the name Vidyānagara to the capital. This is shown in the following table:—

Shimoga	13	inscriptions
Chitaldroog	13	»
Hassan	10	»
Mysore	5	»
Kadūr	4	»
Kolar	4	»
Tumkūr	4	»
Nellore	1	»

1 Burnell, *Elements of South-Indian Palaeography*, p. 26, note 2.

2 Fleet, *Three Copper-plate Grants of the Kings of Vijayanagara*, *J.B.B.R.A.S.*, XII, p. 336.

3 Cf. Basu, *Vijayanagara in Bengal Tradition*, *I.H.Q.*, III, p. 261-263.

10. Accordingly the three districts that have most of those inscriptions are Shimoga, Chitaldroog and Hassan. The focus of such fable is to be found in the middle of these three districts. Now the Kadūr District is almost completely surrounded by these three districts. Hence the original place of the story seems to be the disrict of Kadūr.

11. Against this statement the following objection may be proposed: If the Kadūr District were the original place of the story, it would naturally possess the majority of such inscriptions. But the District of Kadūr has only four inscriptions with the word Vidyānagara. This objection is apparently very weighty, specially if we suppose that the forgers of those early grants and propagators of the story of the foundation of Vijayanagara by Vidyāraṇya were people without knowledge and education. But we cannot suppose such a thing. The fabricators of this fable were very shrewd and very well-educated men, who succeeded in spreading their story throughout the Empire and in obtaining the assent of their contemporaries and successors, and even of historians centuries later. The spreading of such inscriptions in the neighbourhood of its birth-place would have easily discovered the fraud. Their purpose was to spread them throughout the Empire. It was nevertheless natural that the majority of those inscriptions should be found in the neighbouring districts.

12. And now the common legal phrase '*Cui bono*', 'in whose profit' is also to be applied to this case. Who was specially interested in the spreading of such a belief in the Kadūr District? In the westernmost corner of the district there is the Śringeri Jagir, and in it the Śringeri math. For the ascetic dwellers of this math, the story of the foundation of Vijayanagara by one of their former Jagad-gurus would be very profitable. If such a story were once believed through-

out the Empire, they could expect any reward they wanted, any lands that they could be in need of any day from the grateful successors of Harihara I, who had, so they said, been enthroned by the great Vidyāraṇya. The fact that this guru had been connected with the imperial family, *viz.* with Mārapa and Bukka I, gave some historical likelihood to the fable. Moreover the time of confusion subsequent to the overthrow of the first dynasty, seemed the best time for the propagation of such a story. Finally such religious ascetics and recluses psychologically are persons often inclined to fabricate such fables. Their knowledge of what they call absolute reality, acquired only by their practice of asceticism, inclines them to place all other things, whether existing or not existing, whether true or false, on the same level of relative reality. Hence the fabrication of a story which one might derive some profit from—provided no harm should result from the concoction to a third person—is always attractive to such religious recluses.

Hence it may be concluded that the ascetics of the Śringeri math fabricated the story of Vidyāraṇya as the founder of the city and Empire of Vijayanagara, in the beginning of the XVIth century[1]. And it seems most probable that the fabrication of the whole story and the falsification of a great number, if not of all the spurious grants above referred to, was perpetrated during the rule of Rāmachandra Bhārati, who directed the Śringeri math from 1508 to 1560[2]. In fact, there is an inscription of the year 1513, in the Chikmagalur Taluka, recording a grant made by śri-Rāmachandra Bhārati svāmi of the village of "Kūḍuaḷḷi, belonging to us, in the Mēlepāḷu of Vasudhāre-śīme, which Harihara-mahārāya

[1] In p. 8 we have come to the same conclusion through a different way, *viz.* that the story of the hare, connected with the one of Vidyaranya, was a falsification of the time of Achyuta Raya or of Sadasiva Raya.

[2] Cf. Rice, *Mysore*, I p. 380.

when he was protecting the kingdom in peace, granted to our Śringeri math as an offering to Vidyāśaṅkara" [1]. This Vidyāśaṅkara is the famous Vidyātīrtha, one of the predecessors of Vidyāraṇya as head of the Śringeri math. The inscription shows the wish of the Jagad-guru, to show the early relations between the math and the Emperors of Vijayanagara. This was perhaps the first step in this campaign of falsification [2]; the second was to be the story of Vidyāraṇya as the founder of the capital of the Empire [3].

3. THE FOUNDATION OF VIJAYANAGARA ACCORDING TO NUNIZ

After rejecting the legendary stories and forged accounts of the foundation of the great capital of Vijayanagara, it is necessary now to investigate the ancient sources we possess, in order to ascertain who was the founder of that city and in what circumstances the foundation took place. For this purpose the study of the Portuguese chronicle of Nuniz will be most valuable. His account, prior to the narrative of the hare and of Vidyāraṇya, is totally different from any other ancient chronicle of the same event.

---

[1] *Ep. Carn.*, VI, Cm, 88.

[2] In fact the date of this grant, 1513, is doubtful, according to Mr. Rice.

[3] In the list of Sringeri all the gurus succeed each other, excepting the case of Vidyaranya and his immediate predecessor Bharati Krishna-tirtha. Cf. Rice, l. c. Both seem to have ruled together for a long period of time, as their respective dates overlap: Bharati from 1328 to 1380, and Vidyaranya from 1331 to 1386. The fact is that in 1380 Vidyaranya seems, as seen above, to have assumed rulership; and it is at least evident that he was not the Jagad-guru prior to this date. These overlapping dates were undoubtedly put at the time of the falsification of those documents in order to show that Madhava Vidyaranya was already the ruler at Sringeri at the time of the foundation of Vijayanagara, as asserted in the story.

The chronicle of Fernão Nuniz after relating the war of Muhammad Tuglak, 'the king of Delly' in the Deccan proper, says:—

"Up to that time, in all that was (afterwards) the kingdom of Bisnaga (Vijayanagara), no place was populated save only the city of Nagumdym (Ānegondi), in which the king of Bisnagà was then awaiting his destruction, since it was strong, and because he possessed no other citadel but that, which was his Lisbon". Then the chronicler describes the siege of the town by the Afghan army, the flight of the Hindu monarch with his chosen troops to the inner fort, and then continues as follows:—"Then the King of Bisnaga, seeing the determination of the soldiers of the King of Delly that they would never leave the place without making an end of those whom he had with him in the fortress, made a speech to them all, laying before them the destruction that the King of the troops of Delly had caused in his own kingdoms; and how not content with that, he had besieged this fortress, so that now there was nothing for them to look to but death, since already there was no water in the fortress nor anything left to eat. And (he said) that of the fifty thousand men who had been in the city of Nagundy, he had chosen them alone as his companions and true friends, and begged of them that they would hold fast in death to the loyalty which they had borne him in their lives; for he hoped that day to give battle to the King of Delly. Then he said that already there remained to him of his kingdom and lordship nothing but that fortress and the people that were in it, and so he asked them to arm themselves and die with him in battle, giving their lives to the enemy who had deprived them of all their lands. All of them were very content and glad at this, and in a short space were all armed; and after they were so the King made them another speech, saying: 'Before we join battle we have to wage another war with our sons and daughters and wives, for it will not be good that we should allow them to be taken for the use of our enemies'.' And the King said: 'I will be the first to deal with my wife and sons'. At this time, they were all standing at a large open space which was before the citadel, and there by the hand of the King were slain over fifty of his wives and some sons and little daughters: and the same was done with their own hands by all who had wives and sons that could not fight. When these nuptial feasts, so abhorred of all, were fulfilled, they opened the gates of the fortress, and their enemies forthwith entered, and slew all of them except six old men who withdrew to a house. These were made captive and were taken before the King (of Delhi), and the King asked them who they were and how they had escaped and they told them who they were; at which the King greatly rejoiced, because one of them was the minister of the kingdom and another the treasurer, and the others were leading officers in it. They were questioned by the King concerning the treasures of the King of Bisnaga, and such riches as were buried in the vaults of the fortress were delivered up to him; they also gave him an account of the revenues of the kingdom of Bisnaga at that time. When all was known to the King he delivered them to one of his captains, and commanded to make over the bodies of the dead to another captain, and gave orders that the bodies should be burned; and the body of the King, at the request of those six men, was conveyed very honourably to the city of Nagundy. From that time forward that place became a burning-place of the kings. Amongst themselves they still worship this king as a saint.

"As soon as the King had thus fulfilled all his desires, he bade his captains to destroy some villages and towns which had risen against him, and give security to those who sought it of him. After the death of the (Hindu) King, he stayed in that fortress two years, having already for twelve waged war on the kingdom. • He was far from his home, which was more than five hundred leagues distant; and his forces being all scattered, news came to him how all the land which was first gained by him had rebelled. As soon as this was known to the King he sent to collect his people, leaving in this fortress, which was the strongest in the kingdom, abundant provisions for its defence in all circumstances; and he left, for captain and governor of the kingdom Enybiquymelly (Mallik Naib), a Moor, and with him he left many troops, showing much kindness to each one of them separately, giving to each lavish gifts and lands in such way that all were content, and, abandoning forthwith all hope of returning to their country, made there their homes.

"The King having departed to his own kingdom in consequence of the news that had been brought to him, leaving the kingdom of Bisnaga in the power of Meliquy niby (Mallik Naib); when it was known throughout the country how he was out of it, those who had escaped to the mountains, with others who, against their will and through fear had taken oaths of fealty for their towns and villages, rose against the captain Mileque neby (Mallik Naib), and came to besiege him in the fortress, allowing no provisions to go in to him, nor paying him the taxes that had been forced on them. And Meliquy niby, seeing how little profit he could get in this country, and how badly he was obeyed, and how far off was the succour sent by his lord the King, sent quickly to him to tell him how all the land was risen against him, and how every one was lord of what he pleased, and no one was on his side; and that His Highness should decide what he thought best to be done in such a case. And when the King heard this news he took counsel, telling the great people of the realm of the letter and message which he had from Milinebiquy (Mallic Naib), his captain and governor of the kingdom of Bisnaga, and how badly the lords of the land obeyed him; so that each one was king and lord over whomsoever he pleased, as soon as he acquired any power, there being no justice amongst them, nor any one whom they wished to obey. What was it seemed best to them (he asked), and what in such case ought they, and could they, do, so that he should not lose so fair a territory and one so rich, the seizure of which had cost such labour, so much money, and the lives of so many of their fellows? All the councillors decided that the King should command the presence of the six men whom he held captive, and that he should learn from them who was at that time the nearest of kin, or in any way related to the Kings of Bisnaga; and this questioning being done, no one was found to whom by right the kingdom could come, save to one of the six whom he held captive, and this one he who at the time of the destruction of Bisnaga had been minister of the kingdom. He was not related by blood to the kings but only was the principal judge; but (it seemed) good that His Highness should give the kingdom to that one. And this advice pleased the King and them all. At once the six captains were released and set at liberty, and many kindnesses and honours were done them, and the governor was raised to be King and the treasurer to be governor; and he took from them oaths and pledges of their fealty as vassals; and they were at once despatched and sent to their lands with a large following to defend them from any one who should desire to do them an injury. And when these six men had thus finished their journey to the city of Nagundy, they found only the ruined basements of the houses and places peopled by a few poor folk. In a short time, the arrival of Deorão (for so he was called) was known in all the country, and how he had been exalted to be King, with which the people were well content, as men who had felt so deeply their subjection to a lord not of their own faith; and from this man have descended all those who have reigned up to now. And they made great feasts for him, and delivered up to him the lands taken by former kings and lost to them and he was obeyed as king. And when the captain Meliquy niby became aware of this, he was very pleased and contented, and delivered up to him the fortress and kingdom as the King his lord had commanded; and making himself ready with all speed he departed, leaving the land to its proper owner. And after he had gone, King Deorão, entering on his rule, strove to pacify the people and those who had revolted, and to make them safe, and he did them many kindnesses so as to secure their good-will, and travelled about their fortresses and towns. He abandoned the lost lands since he knew that he could not regain them, having no army or forces for such a work, nor any cause for which he could make war; and also because he was very old"[1].

After this Nuniz relates the foundation of the city of Vijayanagara by king Deorão moved by the fact of the hare biting his dogs and advised by the ascetic Vidyāraṇya[2].

This long quotation from the chronicle of Nuniz will help us to study critically his account. He calls it "Copy and Summary of a Cronicle of the Kings of Bisnaga". The Portuguese word '*Sumario*' does not mean the same as the word 'Summary' in Sewell's translation. '*Sumario*' means an account. Hence the narrative of Nunes was not a summarised account of the ancient chronicle which he says he came across during his stay at Vijayanagara, but a full translation of it. This chronicle nevertheless, is not to be

---

1 Sewell, *The Forgotten Empire*, p. 292-298. 2 Ibid., p. 299-301. Both legends have been exploded in the preceding pages.

(*To face p. 41.*)

Facts related by Nuniz.	Corresponding facts in Mussulman History	Hoysala History	Vijayanagara History
The King of Delhi entered the lands of the King of Bisnaga.	Invasion of the Hoysala Empire by Mallik Kafur in 1310 (Ferishta-Briggs, I, p. 373)		
In the city of Ānegondi the King of Bisnaga was awaiting his destruction.		Vira Ballaḷa III waited for the enemy in his capital Dōrasamudra (Ferishta-Briggs, l. c.)	
The King of Delhi had been at war with the king of Bisnaga for twelve years.	Alla-ud-din Khilji had been at war with the Hoysalas since 1310 (Ferishta-Briggs, l. c.)		
Out of the whole army of Ānegondi six nobles remained, who became the founders of Vijayanagara.			Five brothers, Harihara, Kampa, Bukka, Mārappa, and Mudappa are supposed to be the founders of Vijayanagara.
The King of Bisnaga dies in battle against the Muhammadans.		Vira Ballaḷa III is defeated and killed by the Sultan of Madura (Defremery-Sanguinetti, *Voyages d'Ibn Batoutah*, IV, p. 196-198; *Ep. Carn.*, VI, Kd, 75).	
After the death of the Hindu King, the King of Delhi remained in that fortress for two years.	Muhammad Tuglak transfered his capital from Delhi to Daulatabad and remained there for some time. (Ferishta-Briggs, I, p. 419-420).		
Rebellion of the subjects of the King of Delhi in the north, during his stay in the south.	Mallik Beiram Abia rebelled in Multan against Muhammad Tuglak during the latter's stay at Daulatabad (Ferishta-Briggs, I, p. 420-421). Then Mallik Fkhr-ud-din rebelled in the eastern provinces (Ibid., p. 423). Shahu, chief of the mountain Afghans also rebelled in Multan (Ibid., p. 425). &		
The King of Delhi leaves Mallik Naib as Governor of the kingdom of Bisnaga.	Mallik Naib Imad-ul-Mulk is left by Muhammad Tuglak as commander of the army at Warangal (Ferishta-Briggs, I, p. 423).		
Rebellion against the Governor Mallik Naib in the south.	Hasan Kangu rebelled against Mallik Naib at Devgiri, and defeated and killed him (Elliot-Dowson, III, p. 257-258).		
The name of the new Hindu King of Bisnaga, appointed by Muhammad Tuglak is Deorão.		Sewell, *The Forgotten Empire*, p. 298, note 2, says that Deorão stands for Dēva Rāya, 'the general title of the Vijayanagar Kings'. But Harihara I and Bukka I never used such title. On the other hand one may easily disclose in this title the real title of Vira Ballaḷa III, who is often called in the inscriptions Vira Ballaḷa Dēvarāsa. (Cf. *Ep. Carn.*, VI, Cm, 105; and many other inscriptions).	
Deorão, who had been imprisoned by Muhammad Tuglak, is some time after set free and returns to his country.		Vira Ballaḷa III, after being taken prisoner by Mallik Kafur (Ferishta-Briggs, I, p. 373), is sent back to his own kingdom. (*Ep. Carn.*, VII, Sh, 68).	

relied upon without a thorough critical study. The extract quoted above seems at first sight to be rejected, because it seems totally incongruous, *i. e.* one out of which no possible historical information on the founder of Vijayanagara is to be drawn. But after careful consideration one traces throughout the narrative some historical events much mixed up with one another, but which may supply precious historical information about the founder of Vijayanagara.

The opposite table will show these historical facts narrated in Nuniz's chronicle and their corresponding events in the contemporary history of Southern India.

Besides this confusion of historical facts, as evinced in the preceding table, the account of Nuniz contains several evident discrepancies which easily persuade the critic that Nuniz's chronicle is to be carefully studied before being accepted as a reliable historical document. Such discrepancies are, for instance, to speak of the King of Vijayanagara before Vijayanagara existed; that six nobles of the so-called kingdom of Bisnaga (one of them being a minister) are said to have withdrawn to a house during the slaughter of the king and the rest of his army; and that precisely one of these nobles becomes the founder of the Vijayanagara Empire; that Muhammad Tuglak sent a new Hindu King to the south in order to put down the rebellions there against him, the Empire of Vijayanagara being thus founded, at least indirectly, by Muhammad Tuglak.

Yet in the midst of this confusion and misplacement of historical facts, one event stands out clear and uncontradicted by other historical documents. This event is the foundation of the city of Vijayanagara by a king, who had been imprisoned by the Delhi Mussulmans, taken as a prisoner to their northern capital, and then sent back to his country in the south. Does Southern Indian History commemorate any such monarch in the first half of the XIVth century? Ferishta relates that in the year 710 H. E., corresponding to 1310 A.D. Mallik Kafur defeated, 'Bilal Dew Raja of the Carnatic' (Vīra Ballāḷa Dēva Rāya III), 'took him prisoner and ravaged his territory' [1]. But an inscription of the Shimoga Taluka informs us that "after the Turaka war, on the occasion of his son Vīra Ballāḷa Rāya (returning) from Diḷḷi (and) entering the city (on the 6th May, 1313), he released the taxes old and new" [2]. Ballāḷa III therefore was taken prisoner to Delhi and afterwards released by the Sultan. Hence Vīra Ballāḷa III seems to be the king pointed out by Nuniz as the founder of the city of Vijayanagara.

5. CRITICAL STUDY OF FERISHTA'S ACCOUNT.

This conclusion has been arrived at, after studying Nuniz's chronicle independently of any other contemporary source of information. Yet Ferishta's narrative of the reign of Sultan Muhammad Tuglak confirms this conclusion in the most amazing way. This author, after referring to the advance of the Mussulmans in the Deccan, says that "Bilal Dew (Ballāḷa Dēva) convened a meeting of his kinsmen, and resolved, first, to secure the forts of his own country, and then to remove the seat of government among the mountains... Bilal Dew, accordingly, built a strong city upon the frontiers of his dominions, and called after his son Beeja (Vija or Vijaya), to which the word nuggar (nagar), or city, was added, so that it is now known by the name of Beejanuggar (Vijayanagara)" [3]. Let us critically study this extract of the Mussulman chronicler for it is of the utmost importance.

---

[1] Ferishta-Briggs, I, p. 373. Cf. *Ep. Carn.*, V, Hn, 51 and 52.

[2] *Ep. Carn.*, VII, Sh, 68.

[3] Ferishta-Briggs, I, p. 427. Sewell, *The Forgotten Empire*, p. 29. note 2, rejects without further study Ferishta's authority on

Ferishta lived in the second half of the XVIth century. "In his youthful days", he himself says, "he was early inspired with a desire of compiling a history of the conquests of Islam in Hind, and of giving some account of the holy personages who have flourished in this country; but being unable to procure the materials necessary for this purpose at Ahmudnuggar (Ahmadnagar), where he then resided, his wish was not fulfilled; when in the year 998 (A. D. 1589) he proceeded from that city of Beejapoor (Bijapur) and was introduced to the prince who then filled the throne of the latter kingdom" [1]. Bijapur was indeed the best city of the Deccan for obtaining information about Vijayanagara. No other capital of the Bahmāni Sultanates had ever been in such connection with the Hindu Empire, both in war and in peace, as Bijapur. And though at that time the city of Vijayanagara was already abandoned for good, and the court was removed to Penukonda, yet the tradition respecting

this point. "This is in itself absurd", says he, "and carries with it its own refutation. It would be manifestly impossible for the city to be "built" in so short a time, and moreover it would have been sheer waste of time for the Prince to have employed himself in such a way. The sentence was probably introduced merely to account for that city having been built about this period". We have seen that Ferishta agrees with Nuniz as regards this fact. Had Ferishta introduced this merely to account for that city being built about this time, the agreement between both sources, could not be satisfactorily explained. Sewell also supposes that the city was, according to Ferishta, built in a short time. But Ferishta does not say anything about the time employed in building the city. We shall see later on how useful for the Hoysala Empire was the work of building such a city in the northern frontier.

Ibid., p. XLVII.

Vijayanagara was undoubtedly alive in the Adil Shahi capital. Moreover, Ferishta testifies that the generosity of Ibrahim Adil Shah II placed in his hand numerous old chronicles of the ancient Afghan Sultans, which he afterwards extracted in his History, after careful critical study much beyond his age. Among these works there is one, the *Tārīkh-i-Firoz Shāhī* by Ziā-ud-din Barni, which could furnish the chronicler with some information about this point. He therefore had the best oral tradition possible, and the ancient Mussulman chronicles, as the source of his information.

There is nevertheless one slight confusion in his account. Bilal Dew is called by Ferishta 'Raja of the Carnatic'; but he does not identify him with the Rāja of Dwar-Sumoodra (Dōrasamudra), for a little afterwards he speaks of an alliance between Bilal Dew and the Rājas of Maabir and Dwar-Sumoodra[1]. The chronicler most likely did not know that the Raja of the Carnatic, then Ballāḷa III, held his court and capital at Dōrasamudra itself.

In any case, Ballāḷa III is said to have built the city of Vijayanagara calling it after his son, named Beeja or Vijaya. There is an inscription in the Chikmagalur Taluka, of the year 1343, that speaks about the *abisheka* of Ballāḷa III's son. Now, the latter is called Vīra Virūpāksha Ballāḷa Dēva[2]. This is a discrepancy between Ferishta and the Hoysaḷa inscriptions, which nevertheless being well considered, proves the genuineness and veracity of the former. He heard that Ballāḷa III had founded that city calling it after his son's name. But at the time of Ferishta the city was known as Vijayanagara. Hence the Mussulman historian, without further inquiries, supposed that Ballāḷa's son was named Vijaya. But the fact

---

[1] Ibid., p. 427.

[2] *Ep. Carn.*, VI, Cm, 105.

is that Vijayanagara was not the original name of this famous city. Another inscription of the year 1339 records that Vīra-Ballāḷa III "was ruling in happiness in Śrī Vīra Vijaya Vīrūpākshapura as his residential capital"[1]. That this was the city of Vijayanagara with its original name, the name itself evidently discloses. It was called first Vijaya, that is the appellation that has been preserved till the present. But besides the city bore the name of Śrī Vīra Virūpāksha, that is exactly the name of Vīra Ballāḷa III's son[2]. In fact an inscription of the time of Harihara II, dated 1380, gives the name Virūpāksha to the city of Vijayanagara[3]. The temple of Virūpāksha, who was supposed to be the protector deity of the city, is undoubtedly a souvenir of the old name of the city, which for the sake of brevity was practically lost at Ferishta's time[4].

6. THE FIRST KINGS OF VIJAYANAGARA IN NUNIZ'S CHRONICLE AND BALLALA III.

The foundation of the city of Vijayanagara by Vīra Ballāḷa III is confirmed by the study of the history of the further

Ep. Carn., IX, Ht, 43.

The full name of Ballala III's son was most likely Sri Vira Vijaya Virupaksha, though the word Vijaya is omitted in the inscription above referred to. On very few occasions this title is granted to the Emperors of Vijayanagara, and nevertheless some of them also seem to have been called Vijaya, for instance Bukka I *(Ep. Carn.,* XI, Dg, 67*)*, Harihara II(Ibid., 68) and Bukka II (Ibid. 108). ³ *M.A.R.*, 1916, p. 57.

Vijayanagara was not a new name for the Hoysala Emperors. Thus Ballala II after conquering the Haneya fort, made a city named Vijayagiri (*Ep. Carn.*, XI, Mk, 12); the same monarch is once found residing, at Vijayapura "which is Hallavur" (*Ep. Carn.*, V, Cn, 244). The capital itself Dorasamudra is said to be "reckoned as Vijayasamudra" (*Ep. Carn.*, IV, Ng, 29).

kings of Vijayanagara in Nuniz's chronicle. First of all the Portuguese writer says that Deorão "was very old" [1]. This statement is true if it refers to the Hoysaḷa King. Ibn Batuta tells us that at the time of his death in 1342 Ballāḷa III was eighty years old [2]. Hence at this time he was about seventy. If we suppose with Sewell that Deorão is Harihara I, we cannot suppose that his age was so much advanced in years and hence the statement of Nuniz would not be correct. Certainly Harihara seems to have been the eldest son of Saṅgama, and we are not acquainted with the year of his death. But his third brother Bukka's death is to be placed at about 1379 [3]. Now supposing that Bukka died when 80 years old and that his eldest brother was ten years older, in 1332 Harihara would have been at most 43 years old, an age which cannot justify the epithet 'very old' given to the founder of Vijayanagara by Nuniz [4].

Now, studying the succession of the first kings of Vijayanagara in the chronicle of Nuniz, the first four kings mentioned in the chronicle are the following:—

Deorão.
Bucarão.
Pureoyre Deorão.
Ajarão.

Sewell, who does not acknowledge Vīra Ballāḷa at all, is obliged to identify the above four kings as follows:—

Deorão.	Harihara I.
Bucarão.	Bukka I.
Pureoyre Deorão.	Harihara II,
Ajarão.	Bukka II and Dēvarāya I.

1 Sewell, *The Forgotten Empire*, p. 299.
2 Defremery-Sanguinetti, *Les Voyages d'Ibn Batoutah*, IV, p. 198.
3 Cf. Sewell, *The Forgotten Empire*, p. 47.
4 This difficulty was already seen by Suryanarain Rao, o.c., p. 149.

According to this table Harihara II is called by Nuniz Pureoyre, which, as Sewell says, "seems to be a rough Portuguese version of the name Harihara" [1]. This seems to be a derivation too far fetched. Moreover according to Nuniz Pureoyre Deorão struck the first coins in Vijayanagara, a circumstance that does not agree with the findings of Numismatics, and forces Sewell to contradict Nuniz's statement in a footnote:—"This king" says he, "was not the first to coin *pardaos* or pagodas" [2]. This seems to suggest that Pureoyre Deorão, the one who first struck coins in Vijayanagara, must be identified with Bukka I, whose pagodas are known long ago [3]. Besides, the facts attributed to Ajarão, such as his wars against the Muhammadans, his conquest of Goa and his building part of the city of Vijayanagara [4], correspond to Harihara II rather than to Bukka II whose reign was short and not very eventful; the name itself sounds more like Harihara than like Bukka. Hence the identification of the kings of Nuniz's list made by Sewell seems to be wrong. The corresponding kings between the list of the Portuguese chronicle and the genealogical lists of the epigraphical records seem to be the following:—

Deorão.	?
Bucarão	Harihara I
Pureoyre Deorão	Bukka I
Ajarão.	Harihara II

It will at the first sight seem strange that Harihara I should be called Bucarão. Nevertheless the original name of this king seems to have been Hakka, afterwards changed

[1] Ibid., p. 48.
[2] Ibid., p. 301, note 1.
[3] Hultzsch, *The Coins of the Kings of Vijayanagara, Ind. Ant., XX*, p. 302.
[4] Sewell, o. c., p. 301.

into Harihara [1]. This name is not so different from the name Bucarao. More strange is the name Pureoyre; but if we pay attention to the fact that *b* and *p* are often interchanged, we easily discover the name Bukka Raya through the corrupted form Pureoyre. All this confirms the opinion that the king Deorão of the chronicle of Nuniz cannot be other than the Hoysaḷa king Vīra Ballāḷa III.

7. THE FOUNDATION OF VIJAYANAGARA AND THE DEFENCE OF THE HOYSALA EMPIRE.

We have an inscription of the year 1339 recording the presence of Ballāḷa III in the city of Srī Vīra Vijaya Virūpākshapura—named afterwards in a simplified way, Vijayanagara—from where he was ruling the Empire 'in happiness' [2]. There is another inscription in the temple of Virūpāksha, called also Pampāpatī temple, at Hampi, in the ancient city of Vijayanagara, that refers to the Hoysaḷas, as showing thereby that Hampi was within the boundaries of the Hoysaḷa Empire [3]. The intimate relations between Ballāḷa III and Vijayanagara are confirmed by the fact of giving the new city the name of his heir-apparent, as said above. Moreover another son of Vīra Ballāḷa III was given the name of Hampi, probably the most ancient name of Ānegondi. In an inscription of the year 1342 he is called Hampe Vodeyar [4].

Now the study of the circumstances which the Hoysaḷa Empire was then going through will perhaps disclose what was the purpose of Vīra Ballaḷa III in founding the city of

Cf. Rice, *Mysore and Coorg from the Inscriptions*, p. 112.

Ep. Carn., IX, Ht, 43.

A. S. of I., Report, 1907-1908, p. 239, note 2.

Ep. Carn., IV, Yd, 29. This prince is perhaps to be identified with Ballala IV.

Vijayanagara at the north of his Empire, and even perhaps what he was doing there in the year 1339. The first Mussulman invasion of the Hoysala Empire took place in the year 1310[1]. This was the expedition of Mallik Kafur, the general of Alla-ud-din Khilji, the Sultan of Delhi. Mallik successfully conquered Dōrasamudra, the capital of the Hoysaḷa Empire, and carried the Hoysaḷa Emperor, as prisoner of war, to Delhi. Vira Ballaḷa III was actually released three years later; and then a period of great activity commenced for that great monarch. In 1316, his capital Dōrasamudra was already restored to its pristine glory and strength, of which it had been deprived by the Mussulman conquerors[2]. In 1326 another army sent by Muhammad Tuglak of Delhi conquered the city of Warangal, the capital of the Kakatīya Dynasty of Telingana[3]. This fact showed Vīra Ballaḷa that it was absolutely necessary to fortify the northern frontier of his Empire, against any other possible invasion of the Delhi Muhammadans. It was on this occasion that, according to Ferishta, "Bilal Dew convened a meeting of his kinsmen, and resolved, first, to secure the forts of his own country"[4]. After this in 1326 we find him at Unnāmale (Tiruvannāmalai)[5]; this was a strategic point in the easternmost corner of the Hoysaḷa Empire, in the way from Warangal to Madura. Vīra Ballaḷa undoubtedly fortified this place to prevent any possible junction of the Delhi forces with the forces of the Madura Sultan. Some years after, in 1339, we find him, as recorded above, at Vijayanagara. This shows that after fortifying the eastern boundaries of his Empire, the Hoysaḷa

[1] *Ep. Carn.*, V, Hn, 51, 52.
[2] *Ep. Carn.*, III, Md, 100.
[3] Ferishta-Briggs, I, p. 427.
[4] Ibid.
[5] *Ep. Carn.*, IX, DB, 14.

monarch had proceeded to the north in order to strengthen the northern cities and fortresses against any other possible attempt of the Delhi army. One of the cities fortified on this occasion was the newly founded city of Srī Vīra Vijaya Virūpākshapura or Vijayanagara.

7. THE ANCIENT NAMES OF THE CITY OF VIJAYANAGARA.

In the course of this lecture we have come across several ancient names attributed to the city of Vijayanagara, which will be opportune to study before ending it, as a matter intimately connected with the foundation of the city in the first half of the XIVth century.

The ancient names given to the city in the inscriptions are these: Hampe, Ānegondi, Hastināvati or Hastini, Kuñjarakōṇa or Kuñjarakōṇa-puri. Some of these forms at least, if not all, are in the inscriptions identified with the word Vijayanagara. Thus in an inscription of the time of Harihara II, dated 1395, he is called "the supreme lord of the royal city Hastināpura-Vijayanagara"[1]. And another inscription of the year 1432 states that Dēva Rāya II "was in the residence of Hampe-Hastināvati, which is Vijayanagari"[2]. Accordingly Mr. Fleet said many years ago that Vijayanagara "was re-established as a capital by the brothers Harihara I and Bukkarāya"[3].

Nevertheless there are other inscriptions that seem to be a little more accurate and do not completely identify Vijayanagara with that ancient town. Thus an inscription of 1399 says that Harihara II "was in the residence of Vijayanagari in the Hastināvati fort"[4]. And in another inscription of the

---

[1] *Ep. Carn.*, VIII, Sb, 103. [2] *Ep. Carn.*, V, Cn, 241.

[3] Fleet, *Three Copper-plate Grants of the Kings of Vijayanagara*, *J. B. B. R. A. S.*, XII, p. 336.

[4] *Ep. Carn.*, VIII, Tl, 71.

year 1420 Dēvā Rāya is said to be "in the residence of Vidyānagari belonging to Ānegondi-durga, which is Hampe-Hastināvati"[1]. Hence Hampe and Hastināvati are different names of Ānegondi, and Vijayanagara is said to be in Ānegondi. This does not mean that Vijayanagara was a kind of a suburb of Ānegondi. Rather Ānegondi was a suburb of Vijayanagara. "The granite piles of a bridge over the river", says Sewell, "or stones marking the limit of the causeway, are to be seen opposite Hampi"[2]. Yet Vijayanagara in the beginning of its existence was said to be in, or to belong to Ānegondi out of respect for the ancient town on the northern bank of the Tuṅgabhadrā. That Kuñjarakōṇa or Kuñjarakōṇa-puri is another name of the city of Ānegondi is evident from the inscriptions themselves. There it is said that Harihara "ruled the whole earth at the city of Kuñjarakōṇa"; and then when going hunting, he "crossed the Tuṅgabhadrā" and met with the marvellous event of the hare in the site of the future Vijayanagara[3]. Evidently therefore Ānegondi and Kuñjarakōṇa are the same city.

Philology confirms this identification. Hastināvati seems to be the Sanskrit form of Ānegondi, *i. e.* 'Elephant Pit'[4]. The same is to be said of the name Kuñjarakōṇa[5]. Hampe or

---

1 *Ep. Carn.*, VII, Sk, 288.

2 Sewell, *Lists of Antiquarian Remains*, I, p. 106.

3 Butterworth, *Nellore Inscriptions*, I, p. 114; *Ep. Carn.*, X, Bg, 70.

4 Cf. Fleet, o. c., p. 336.

5 Butterworth, o. c., I, p. 114. Mr. Suryanarain Row, *The Never To Be Forgotten Empire*, p. 139, note*, says that Anegondi does not mean 'Elephant Pit', but 'Elephant Lane'. "If, as Mr. Rice conjectures", he adds, "it was an 'Elephant Pit', then the Sanskritists were wrong in having translated it into Hastinapura, or Hastinavati". This statement seems to be a little too hasty, for the Sanskrit word *avat* also means a well or a cistern, which are nothing else than a pit. In the same way the Sanskrit *kona*, of the word Kunjarakona means a corner, that has a slight different connotation.

Hampi is nothing else but the Kanarese form of the ancient Sanskrit name Pampā spoken of in the Mahābhārata. Hence it is probable that this word is the oldest name of the city[1].

How old the city itself is, it is difficult to say. "The exact age of the earliest settlement at Hampi is as yet unknown", says Mr. Sewell. "It is said that a town existed there as early as A. D. 1100"[2]. Fergusson—not a great authority in chronology—gives the year 1118 as the year of the foundation of the first city of Vijayanagara by one Vijaya Rayal[3]. According to Mr. Suryanarain Row—who seems to derive his information from the *Rāya Vaṁśavali* of the ancient kings of Ānegondi— the first king of Ānegondi was Nanda Mahārāja, whose rule commenced in 1014; but in 1150 the then ruling monarch Vijayadhwaja transferred the capital to the other side of the Tuṅgabhadrā thus becoming the founder of the early city of Vijayanagara[4]. All these statements however seem to be totally groundless. The fact is that the temple of Virūpāksha on the southern bank of the Tuṅgabhadrā existed in 1237, one century before Harihara I settled there[5].

What was the kingdom the capital of which was Ānegondi it is not an easy thing to say. Mr. Gopinatha Rao says that "two inscriptions. . . state that Harihara I was a chieftain reigning over Navakhaṇḍa with Kuñjarakuṇa as his capital"[6]; but these inscriptions referred to by him do not mention Navakhanda at all. Sometimes inscriptions of

---

1 Fleet, o. c., p. 337.

2 Sewell, *Lists of Antiquarian Remains*, I, p. 106.

3 Fergusson, *History of Indian and Eastern Architecture,* p. 374. (London, 1876).

4 Suryanarain Row, o. c., p. 11 and 12.

5 *A. S. of I., Report,* 1925-26, p. 140.

6 Gopinatha Rao, *Srisailam Plates of Virupaksha, Ep. Ind.*, XV, p. 10.

the Vijayanagara rulers speak of 'the kingdom of Hastināvati', or 'of Hampe-Hastināvati', or 'Hampe', or 'of Ānegondi'. Hence this was most likely the appellation of the kingdom. Thus an inscription of 1379-80 speaks of "the District of Gadag, which is also called the wealthy Kratupura, situated in the middle of the country of Śrī-Toragal, which is in the kingdom of Hastināvati"[1].

The sovereigns of this kingdom of Hastināvati are not well known. Mr. Suryanarain Row gives a list of 10 kings mentioned in the *Rāya Vaṁśāvali*, in the possession of the present Raja of Anegondi[2]. But the *Vaṁśāvali* is so confused with accounts about other more or less contemporary families, for instance about the Chalukyas, the Kalachurris and the Hoysaḷas, that there can be no doubt about its concoction. Moreover, the story of Vidyāraṇya, nicely attached to the end of the *Vaṁśāvati* confirms the fabrication of the whole document.

Mr. Sewell speaks of another king called Kapa Mahārāja "who preceded the Vijayanagara kings" and who according to tradition built the original fort of Gandikota, afterwards restored and strengthened by one of the two Hariharas[3]. This king however is found neither in the above *Vaṁśāvali* nor in any of the published inscriptions.

According to the Dharmakarta of the Pampāpatī temple at Hampi "there are inscriptions and records extant to prove that the great gōpura of the first prākāra of the Hampi temple was originally built in A. D. 1199, when a certain 'Bodayya Rāja' gave the village of Hampi as a charitable gift for the use of the temple"[4]. Yet such records

---

1 *J. B. B. R. A. S.*, XII, p. 377.
2 Suryanarain Row, o. c., p. i.
3 Sewell, *Lists of Antiquarian Remains*, I, p. 123.
4 Ibid., p. 106.

and inscriptions had never been published, and are consequently quite doubtful. Such a king is absolutely unknown, unless he is the same Bodha Mahādēva, who was on the throne of Durga two centuries after, in 1371, "at the time that Bukka Rāya was ruling the kingdom of the world in peace and wisdom"[1]. If such is the case, those inscriptions and records are to be declared spurious.

There is moreover a series of grants that are not genuine, of several of the well known kings of Vijayanagara dated one or two centuries before their existence, as if pretending to spread the belief that the ancient kings of Ānegondi were of the same family as the kings of Vijayanagara. There exists for instance a grant of Vijaya Bukka Rāja dated 1187[2]; another of Śrī Pratāpa Vijaya Bukka Rāja of the same date[3]; a third one of the Mahāmaṇḍalēśvara Harihara of the year 1297[4]; and there is still a fourth one of the year 1354 made by Vijaya Bukka Rāya, Narasa Rāya and Śrī Kṛishṇa Rāya together[5]. The subject of the Rājas of Ānegondi seems to have been a most attractive subject to grant-forgers and king-fabricators. Just last May while at Kēladi, Sagar Taluka, I was shown a single copper-plate grant by one of the priests of the temple, whose ancestors, so he says, had originally come from Ānegondi. The plate was very roughly engraved and at once roused my suspicion. After knowing its contents, those suspicions became certanty: the plate recorded a grant of lands to the ancestors of the priest made by the king of Ānegondi Achyuta Raya, father of Veṅkaṭadri, in Śaka 1054, corresponding to the year 1132.

---

1 *Ep. Carn.*, VI, Mg, 87.

2 Sewell, o. c., p. 117.

3 Ibid., p. 118.

4 *Ep. Carn.*, I, Cg, 59.

5 Sewell, o. c., p. 112.

Three inscriptions of the Shikarpur Taluka speak of one Emperor Janamējaya, who "was in Hastināpura, ruling the kingdom in peace and wisdom". He is said to be "the son of the Emperor Parīkshit". Some of his *birudas* are like those of the Vijayanagara Emperors, but the majority are totally different, for instance: "bestower of widowhood on the wives of hostile kings" or "tanner of the deer the feudatories" or "daily terrifier of the four-quarters of Konkaṇa". He is spoken of as directing "an expedition of victory to the South"[1]. Everything seems genuine in these three inscriptions but for the date: it corresponds to 3102 B.C. in the three records. Mr. Rice calculates the date as 1192 A.D., and is of opinion that they are a much later fabrication, framed on an inscription of Vīra Noḷamba of the Nolamba Dynasty[2].

There are only two genuine inscriptions that mention one of the ancient kings of Ānegondi. These are two inscriptions of Bukka I dated 1355 and 1356, which speak of Hosapaṭṭana (Vijayanagara) as "the capital of Nijagali Kaṭaka Raya"[3]. Evidently this was a well known person in the time of Bukka, perhaps the most famous king of the kingdom of Hastināvati.

All these details seem to point to the fact that there was no city at all on the southern banks of the Tuṅgabhadrā in the beginning of the XIVth century; the temple of Virūpāksha mentioned above being perhaps the only building existing there when the city of Vijayanagara was founded. Accordingly Ballaḷa III was the real founder of the city of Śrī Vīra Vijaya Virūpākshapura, which eventually became Vijayanagara not long after. Anyhow Ānegondi or Hastināvati

---

[1] *Ep. Carn.*, VII, 12, 45, 86.

[2] *Ep. Carn.*, IX, Bn, 142. Cf. Rice, *Mysore and Coorg*, p. 58, note 2.

[3] Rice, *Mysore Inscriptions*, p. 2 and 4.

was always considered as the nucleus of the new town, out of respect for its glorious past.

8. VIJAYANAGARA CALLED HOSAPATTANA.

In connection with the foundation of Vijayanagara the word Hosapaṭṭana, found in some of the inscriptions of the Vijayanagara sovereigns, deserves our special attention. Thus inscriptions of the years 1354 and 1355 say that Bukka I's capital was Hosapaṭṭana [1]. Accordingly other inscriptions of later years testify that he was ruling in Hosapaṭṭana [2], or call him "the great chieftain of Hosapaṭṭana [3]. Where was this city? Was it the same as Vijayanagara?

The fact is that all the inscriptions mentioned above state that Hosapaṭṭana was "in the Hoysaṇa country"; and this is a stumbling block for Mr. Rice: "Sir Walter Elliot says (*Num. Or.*, 91) that the first name of Vijayanagar was Hosapaṭṭana", declares Mr. Rice, "which is quite possible, as the word merely means New Town. But that would not be in the Hoysaṇa country"[4]. Such is Mr. Rice's statement. Prescinding from the opinion of Sir Walter Elliot, which will be referred to later on, it is beyond doubt that the southern banks of the Tuṅgabhadrā formed part of the Hoysaḷa Empire. One of the early Hoysaḷa Emperors Vinayāditya is called "the ornamental head of the Kuntala dominion on the earth" [5]. It is therefore clear that the Kuntala country was within the Hoysaḷa Empire from the early years of the dynasty. Now in the year 1430 an inscription of Dēva Rāya II testifies that the city of Vijayanagara is situated in the Kun-

---

[1] *A.S. of I., Report*, 1907-8, p. 240, note 3; *J.B.B.R.A.S.*. XII, p. 339.
[2] Rice, l. c.; *Ep. Carn.*, XI, Cd, 2, 3.
[3] Fleet, *P. S. O. C. I.*, p. 21, No 149 and No. 150.
[4] Rice, *Ep. Carn.*, IX, p. 24.
[5] *M.A.R.*, 1923, p. 35.

tala country [1]. Another inscription of Achyuta Rāya, dated 1538, similarly states that the city of Vidyānagara *(sic)* "belonged to the government of the Kuntala-dēśa" [2]. The same is said in another inscription of Sadāśiva of the year 1555 [3]. Hence Vijayanagara was also included in the Hoysaḷa Empire, and could therefore be said to form part of the Hoysaṇa country. Consequently Hosapaṭṭana may be the same as Vijayanagara [4].

That they were actually the same is quite clear if the inscriptions of Bukka I are carefully examined. One states that Bukka I "inhabited the city that bore the name of Vijaya, just as Mukunda (Vishnu=Kṛishṇa) inhabited the charming Dvarāvati" [5]; and another says that Bukka made Vijayanagara "his permanent metropolis" [6]. Hence Hosapaṭṭana, so often mentioned as the residence of Bukka I, cannot but be Vijayanagara itself. Now, according to Sir Walter Elliot, Hosapaṭṭana should be the oldest name of Vijayanagara called New City to distinguish it from the old city of Hampe-Hastināvati. It has already been seen that the first official name given to the new city was Śrī Vīra Vijaya Virūpākshapura. In any case Hosapaṭṭana should be a popular name. Now it is a fact that the form Hosapaṭṭana does not appear in the inscriptions of Harihara I. In one of his inscriptions of the year 1340, found very recently, Hosa-Hampeya-Paṭṭaṇa is only mentioned [7]. Hence Vijayanagara in the

1 *Ep. Carn.*, XI, Cd, 29.
2 Ibid., 45.
3 Ibid., Cl, 54.
4 In spite of this Dr. Shamasastry identifies Hosapattana with Sakrepatna. Cf. *M.A.R.*, 1927, p. 62.
5 *J.B.B.R.A.S.*, XII, p. 373.
6 *Ep. Carn.*, II, p. 115, note 9.
7 *South-Indian Epigraphy Report*, 1927, p. 112, No. 88.

time of Harihara I was popularly called Hosa-Hampeya Paṭṭana, New City of Hampe. There is another inscription of the year 1333 stating that Ballāḷa III was ruling in Hosabeṭṭa[1]. Can this name refer to the same Hosa-Hampeya-Paṭṭana? There is therefore no doubt that in the time of Harihara Vijayanagara was called New City. But is there any satisfactory explanation of the word Hosapaṭṭana so often given to Vijayanagara in the time of Bukka I?

One of the inscriptions of Bukka I of the year 1356 informs us that his kingdom was "growing by the benedictions of the good"[2]. It seems indeed that Bukka I's kingdom was soon much extended not only by the benedictions of the good but also, and specially, by the strength of his arm and the valour of his sons and generals. "Having conquered the whole world", continues another of his inscriptions, "he built a splendid city called the city of victory"[3]. This city of victory evidently is the same founded by Vīra Ballaḷa III, called afterwards Vijayanagara. The meaning of this phrase, therefore, is not precisely that Bukka built a new city, but that he so enlarged and beautified the old one that he may be said in some way to have built a new capital. The effect produced by this extension of the capital over his subjects was so great that this is the only occasion in which Bukka is given the title of Mahārājadhirāja. It seems that even a new great ceremony of enthronement took place after the new extension was finished; for the inscription expressly mentions king Bukka' s "mounting the great throne of the new Vijayanagara"[4]. This seems to have happened in 1368, *viz.* thirteen years after he succeed-

---

[1] *Ep. Carn.*, IX, Nl, 9.

[2] *Ep. Carn.*, X, Lr, 222.

[3] *Ep. Carn.*, V, Cn, 256.

[4] *Ep. Carn.*, VII, Sk, 281.

ed his brother Harihara. Such an event seems to have produced an enormous impression upon all. More than a century and a half after Couto, the Portuguese historian, heard of it and according to this information he wrote in his chronicle that king Bukka "founded Visaya Nagar" [1].

One of the inscriptions that speaks of this great event gives a fine poetical description of the new town, the Hosapaṭṭana: "Its fort walls were like arms stretching out to embrace Hēmakūṭa. The points of the battlements like its filaments, the suburbs like its blossom, the elephants like bees, the hills reflected like stems in the water of the moat, the whole city resembled the lotus on which Lakshmī is ever seated. There, with the Tuṅgabhadrā as his footstool, and Hēmakūṭa as his throne, he (Bukka) was seated like Virūpāksha for the protection of the people of the earth"[2].

It may now be asked whether the name of the town of Hospet is perhaps a corruption of the old name Hosapaṭṭana of the times of Bukka. To give a suitable reply to this question it is necessary to recollect a fact of the reign of Kṛishṇa Dēva Rāya. Fernão Nuniz after speaking of a love affair between this king and a dancing girl, whom he seems to have married later on, says the following:—

"This king built a city in honour of this woman, for the love he bore her, and called its name Nagallapor and surrounded it with a new wall which is one of the best works that he has in his kingdom, and he made in it a street very long and large with houses all of masonry. In order to people this town he ordered all the chiefs of his kingdom to build themselves palaces therein, and so they did. This town has one principal street of length four thousand and seven hun-

[1] According to Sewell, p. 222.
[2] *Ep. Carn.*, Cn, 256.

dred paces (about a mile and a quarter) and of breadth forty, which is certainly the most beautiful street it is possible to see; and he made and finished this town without stinting any expense on it"[1]. This city was within the outer walls of Vijayanagara, and consequently formed one of its suburbs. "This new city that the king made", says Paes, who saw Kṛishṇa Rāya himself living in it, "bears the name of his wife for love of whom he made it"[2]. Nagalapur therefore was the official name. This nevertheless was soon apparently forgotten; in order to distinguish this suburb from the main old town, the people used to call it " the new city". Nuniz, who pretends to write a historical chronicle, gives the official name Nagalapur, while writing in the time of Achyuta Dēva Rāya. But Paes, who does not intend to write history, but only an every-day diary, full of his own personal experiences and observations, does not give the official name of this city at all, in spite of writing at the time of Kṛishṇa Dēva Rāya himself. Yet he has kept in his diary the popular name of the town: when he speaks of it he always calls it "the new city"[3], that is Hosapattana or simply Hospet.

It is therefore proved that in the time of Harihara I Vijayanagara was popularly called Hosa-Hampeya Paṭṭana. In the time of Bukka I the city received the name of Hosapaṭṭana; and finally one of the suburbs of Vijayanagara built later on by Kṛishṇa Dēva Rāya was also called by the people Hospet, a denomination that has been kept down to our days.

[1] Sewell, p. 363.
[2] Ibid., p. 246.
[3] Ibid., and p. 283.

PART II

The Origin of the Saṅgama Dynasty

1. THE SUPPORTERS OF THE TELUGU ORIGIN

The first to my knowledge who published any statement about this interesting point was Mr. Francis Buchanan, who in 1807, while extracting the account of the rulers of Tuluva, as given him by the Brahman Ramuppa Varmika (Ramappa Varmika), says referring to the Emperors ot Vijayanagara: "They were of Andray or Telinga descent"[1]. Ramappa seems not to have given any proof of this statement; and his whole account is so full of contradictions and confusion that it deserves no more attention than a passing reference.

After Buchanan, Col. Mark Wilks repeated the same view of the Tuluva origin of the first Vijayanagara dynasty. After narrating the capture of the city of Warangal by the Afghan army and the subversion of the Kākatīya dynasty, Wilks continues as follows: - "Two illustrious fugitives, Booka (Buka) and Aka Hurryur (Harihara), officers of the treasury of the dethroned king of Warankul (Warangal), warned by one of those sacred visions which precedes, or is feigned to precede, the establishment of every Hindoo empire, formed the project of a new government, to be fixed on the banks of the river Toombudra (Tuṅgabhadrā), a

[1] Buchanan, *A Journey from Madras*, III, p. 113.

southern branch of the Kistna (Kṛishṇa), under the spiritual and temporal guidance of the sage Videyarannea (Vidyāraṇia). This capital named Videyanuggur (Vidyānagara = Vijayanagara), in compliment to their minister and preceptor, was commenced in 1336 and finished in 1343. Aka Hurryhur reigned until 1350, and Booka until 1378". And then he dogmatically concludes:—"This origin of the new government at once explains the ascendency of the Telinga language and nation at this capital of Carnatic... The government founded by foreigners was also supported by foreigners; and in the centre of Canara, a Telinga court was supported by a Telinga army" [1]. Wilks does not give any reference to any source from whence he drew all this information. But we suspect that all this theory was concocted to explain the Telugu language and army of the rulers of the last Dynasty of Vijayanagara, the Āravīḍu, who certainly were of Telugu descent.

Mr. H. H. Wilson in the Introduction to his *Mackenzie Collection* does not give his opinion about the origin of this Dynasty, but mentions the different legends about the same, after stating the following:—"The foundation of the state of Vijayanagar is very generally admitted to have arisen out of the subversion of the Hindu Governments of the Kakateya and Belala Rajas by the incursions of the Mohammedans in the beginning of the fourteenth century"[2]. The same is done by Mr. Sewell in his classical work on Vijayanagara [3]; but at the end he states that the "two brothers (Harihara and Bukka), Hindus of the Kuruba caste, who were men of strong religious feeling, serving in the treasury of the king of Warangal, fled from that place on its sack and de-

---

1 Wilks, *Historical Sketches of the South of India*, I, p. 13-14.

2 Wilson, *The Mackenzie Collection*, p. 83 (Calcutta, 1882).

3 Sewell, *A Forgotten Empire*, p. 21-22.

struction in 1323, and took service under the petty Rājah of Ānegundi"[1]. Mr. Suryanarain Row also seems inclined to admit the Telugu origin of the family[2]. Finally Mr. Vincent Smith says the following: — "Good authority exists for regarding the brothers as fugitives from the eastern Telinga or Telegu kingdom of Warangal"[3].

It is not strange therefore that Mr. V. Rangachari, following the steps of those early writers, and in order to explain the Telugu invasions into Southern India (which mostly took place during the rule of the Āraviḍu Emperors), should make this assertion several years after:—"The Rajas of Vijayanagara were probably Telugus, though their capital was in the Canarese country"[4]. And even Mr. Lewis Rice, the eminent epigraphist of Mysore, while speaking of the founders of Vijayanagara, says the following:—"They may have descended from feudatories either of the Hoysaḷa Ballaḷas or of Pratāpa Rudra of the Kākaṭeya family"[5].

All these authors do not give any proof of their assertions, except the one that there were Telugu expeditions into the southernmost part of the Indian continent; but this does not prove much as regards the first dynasty. Anyhow there is a copper-plate grant which could be used to prove the supposed Telugu nationality of the Saṅgama dynasty. This is the Bitragunta grant of Saṅgama II, a nephew of Bukka I and of Harihara I. The inscription is in Sanskrit verse, but

[1] Ibid., p. 23.

[2] Suryanarain Row, *The Never To Be Forgotten Empire*, p. 19 and 148.

[3] Smith, *Oxford History of India*, p. 301 (Oxford, 1923).

[4] Rangachari, *The History of the Naik Kingdom of Madura*, *Ind. Ant.*, XLIII, p. 113.

[5] Rice, *Mysore and Coorg*, I, p. 223.

the characters are Telugu[1]. Such an epigraphical record of one of the early members of the family in Sanskrit written in Telugu characters would certainly mean something, but for the country Saṅgama II ruled over as Viceroy. His father Kampa had already ruled the Udayagiri-rājya in the Telugu country[2]; and Saṅgama himself was holding sway over a portion of the Telugu country, as Kampa's successor, from the capital Vikramāsiṁhapura[3]. This grant being for the Telugu country, it is but natural that its script should be Telugu. This, nevertheless, is an isolated instance in those early days; for we may affirm with Rice that "the earliest of the inscriptions of the Vijayanagar kings are found in the north and west of Mysore"[4]. There is besides an old MS. entitled *Rājakālanirṇaya* that also refers to the Telugu origin of the Saṅgama family, by making Harihara and Bukka the keepers of the records of Vīra Rudra of Warangal[5]. This account nevertheless seems quite untenable on account of several discrepancies; one of them is for instance that after the defeat of the Kākatīya king of Warangal, both brothers are presented in alliance with the northern Mussulmans waging war against Ballaḷa III. In any case even Mr. Gopinatha Rao, who seems to accept this alliance with the Muhammadans[6], does not hesitate in stating that the *Rājakālarnirṇaya* "is not of any historical value"[7].

On the other hand the mediaeval Russian traveller

[1] H. Krishna Sastri, *Bitragunta Grant of Sangama II, Ep. Ind.*, III, p. 21.
[2] Butterworth, *Nellore Inscriptions*, II, p. 789.
[3] H. Krishna Sastri, l. c., p. 33.
[4] Rice, l. c.
[5] Gopinatha Rao, *Srisailam Plates of Virupaksha, Ep. Ind.*, XV, p. 10.
[6] Suryanarain Row, o. c., p. 11.
[7] Ibid., p. 10.

Nikitin, who was in India towards the close of the first Vijayanagara Dynasty, speaks of "the Hindoo Sultan Kadam", who resided at "Bichenegher" (Vijayanagara)[1]. From these words Mr. Sewell concludes that Nikitin "seems to favour the view that they belonged to the old royal house of the Kadambas of Banavâse"[2]. In fact several years before Mr. Lewis Rice had also announced the probable theory that the Sangaṁa family were connected with the Kadambas[3].

The study of contemporary sources will perhaps disclose the real origin of this dynasty.

2. THE ENTHRONEMENT OF HARIHARA I BY VIRA BALLALA III OF THE HOYSALA-VAMSA.

In the previous lecture it has been proved that Vīra Ballaḷa III was the founder of the city of Vijayanagara with the name of Vīra-Vijaya-Virūpâkshapura. Now, if we carefully examine the inscriptions of this monarch, we shall realize that in the later years of his reign he had not a fixed residence, as his predecessors, but he frequently changed his capital, according to the needs of the Empire, and in order to secure its defence against the Mussulmans. These changes will be seen in the following table:—

Changes of Residence of Ballaḷa III
from 1299 to 1343.

Year	Capital	Inscription
1299	Dōrasamudra	*Ep. Carn.*, IX, Kl, 76.
1318	Aruṇasamudra	Ibid., Cn, 73.
1319	Dōrasamudra	Ibid., Kl, 68.
		Ibid., Cn, 12.
		Ep. Carn., XII, Tm, 63.

---

1 Nikitin, *India in the Fifteenth Century*, p. 29 (Hakluyt So.).
2 Sewell, *A Forgotten Empire*, p. 22.
3 Rice, *Mysore Inscriptions*, p. XXXVI.

Year	Capital	Inscription
1328	Dōrasamudra	*Ep. Carn.*, XII, Tm, 55.
	Uṇṇāmalepaṭṭaṇa	*Ep. Carn.*, IX, DB, 14 and 18.
		Ibid., 1.
		Ep. Carn., IX, Ht, 124.
	Uraṇṇāmalepaṭṭaṇa	Ibid., Dl, 60.
1330	Virūpāksha-paṭṭana	*Ep. Carn.*, V, Ak, 66.
1333	Hosabeṭṭa	*Ep. Carn.*, IX, Nl, 9.
1334	Dōrasamudra	*Ep. Carn.*, IX, Cn, 7.
1339	Vīra Vijaya Virūpākshapura	*Ep. Carn.*, IX, Ht, 43.
1340	Hosanāḍ	*Ep. Carn.*, IX, DB, 13.
	Uṇṇāmalepaṭṭaṇa	*Ep.Carn.*, IX, Dl, 54.
		Ibid., Bn, 31.
1342	In the city of Uṇṇāmale	*Ep. Carn.*, IX, Bn, 129.
	In the city of Uṇṇāmale	*Ep. Carn.*, IX, Dl, 46.
	Uṇṇamālepaṭṭaṇa	*Ep. Carn.*, IX, Ht, 147.
	Uṇṇamāle	*Ep. Carn.*, IX, Bn, 24.
1342	Virūpākshapāda	*Ep. Carn.*, IX, Dv, 21.
	Uṇṇāmalepaṭṭaṇa	*Ep. Carn.*, IX, Bn, 21.
1343	Uṇṇāmalepaṭṭaṇa	*Ep. Carn.*, IX, Bn, 41.

The first change of capital, according to the above table, took place in 1328, when Ballaḷa transferred his residence from Dōrasamudra to Uṇṇāmalepaṭṭaṇa, i.e. Tiruvaṇṇāmalai. This date seems to coincide with the conquest of Warangal by the Mussulmans and the meeting of Krishna Nāyaka with Ballaḷa III referred to by Ferishta[1]. It was therefore most likely at Tiruvaṇṇāmalai that the assembly of Ballaḷa III with

[1] Ferishta-Briggs, I, p. 427.

his kinsmen in order to defend the Empire against the Muhammadans was held. The fortification of the northern frontier was there decided; and in fact in the year 1330 we find Ballaḷa III at Virūpāksha-paṭṭaṇa (Vijayanagara). There he remains for 10 years down to 1340, if we except a short visit to Dōrasamudra in 1334. During all this period Ballaḷa seems to have been at the head of his army ready to offer battle to his enemies, the Muhammadans. In 1330 a grant was made in the Hoskote Taluka "for success to the sword and arm of Vira Vallaḷa-Dēvar [1]". Two years later another inscription refers to Siṅge-deṇṇāyakkar, the son (nephew) of Ballāḷa III himself, and generalissimo of an army, whose three officers are also mentioned [2].

It is therefore evident that those changes of capital and these wars were intimately connected with each other, and both were directly intended to secure the defence of the Empire.

And it was most likely at this time, in the period running from 1330 to 1340, — the traditional date of the foundation of Vijayanagara, 1335-6, being between these two dates—that Harihara I was enthroned at Vijayanagara by the old Hoysaḷa monarch as his own mahāmandalēśvara in the north. This is not a groundless surmise, because for a period of some years we trace both chiefs, the Emperor and his mahāmandalēśvara, acting in mutual understanding. In 1336 Harihara seems to have built a fort at Bārakūru (Barkūr)[3]. Two years later Vīra Ballaḷa himself "paid a visit to the Bārakūr army" [4]. This visit seems to be a visit of inspect-

[1] *Ep. Carn.*, IX, Ht, 100.
[2] Ibid., 104.
[3] Cf. Sturrock, *South Kanara Manual*, I, p. 55.
[4] *Ep. Carn.*, V, Ak, 183.

ion to the newly constructed fortification by his mahāmandalēśvara Harihara. One year after, in 1339, we find Vīra Ballaḷa at Vijayanagara itself, as stated above; and in 1340 a fort was being built at Badāmi by one Chamarāja, a Nāyak of Harihara I, who is accordingly called 'the glorious mahāmandalēśvara' [1]. These isolated instances of the activities of Harihara prove that the unity in ideals and plans that existed between Harihara and his paramount lord was the defence of the northern frontier against the Muhammadans [2]. As a matter of fact, Harihara was so successful that in the year 1342, he was, according to Ibn Batuta, acknowledged by the Mussulman chief of Honāvar [3]. This success of his mahāmandalēśvara in the north freed Ballaḷa of any fear of a new invasion from Delhi, and thus an inscription of 1341 could truly say that Ballaḷa "was pleased to rule the earth in peace" [4]. It was then that Vīra Ballaḷa III turned his arms against the other enemy to the south-east of his Empi-

[1] Fleet, *Sanskrit and Old Canarese Inscriptions, Ind. Ant.*, X, p. 63.

[2] Mr. H. Krishna Sastri, *The First Vijayanagara Dynasty, A.S. of I., Report*, 1907-8, p. 236, says that "perhaps the change of capital by Ballala III from Dhorasamudra to Tiruvannamalai was due not only to the fear of the Muhammadans, but also to the rising power of his feudatory chiefs Harihara I and Bukka I". This is a totally unfounded supposition contradicted by the above facts.

[3] Ibn Batuta states that the chief of Hinaur (Honavar), called Djemal-addin Mohammed (Jamal-ud-din Muhammad), "is under the sovereignty of a heathen monarch named Hariab (Hariyappa *or* Harihara)". Defremery—Sanguinetti, o. c., IV, p. 68. In many inscriptions Harihara I receives the name of Hariyapa or Hariyappa. Cf. *Ep. Carn.*, IV, Ch, 64; V, Bl, 3; Cn, 256; VIII, Sb, 104, 110; Tl, 154; IX, DB, 66a; Bn, 47, 59, 73, 97; X, Sg, 112; Mr, 39; *M. A. R.*, 1913-14, p. 46; 1916, p. 56.

[4] *Ep. Carn.*, X, Mr, 82.

re; and he met with a glorious death in the same year 1342 while fighting with the Madura Sultan Ghiyath-ud-din [1].

After reaching this stage of our study, it naturally occurs to ask: Who was this successful chief Harihara, placed by Vīra Ballaḷa as his mahāmandalēśvara in the northern frontier of his Empire, in the most responsible post against the Muhammadans?

3. WHO WAS SANGAMA, THE FATHER OF HARIHARA.

Harihara is said to be the son of one Saṅgama. His mother is not always mentioned. A stone inscription of Bellur gives her name as Śāradā [2]. But other inscriptions call her Mālāmbikā [3], Manāmbikā [4], Gaurāmbikā [5], Gālāmbikā [6], Kāmambikā [7], Kāmāyi [8], and Kāmākshī [9]. Saṅgama himself also receives several names: Sangama [10], Saṅgama [11], Saṁgama [12],

1 Defremery-Sanguinetti, o. c., IV, p. 198.
2 Rice, *Mysore Inscriptions*, p. 227; *Ep. Carn.*, V, Bl, 3.
3 *Ep. Carn.*, X, Gd, 46; Mb, 158.
4 *Ep. Carn.*, X, Bg, 70.
5 *Ep. Carn.*, VII, Ci, 13.
6 Butterworth, *Inscriptions of the Nellore District*, I, p. 113.
7 *Ep. Carn.*, VIII, Sb, 375.
8 *Ep. Carn.*, IV, Ch, 64.
9 *Ep. Ind.*, III, p. 228; VIII, p. 305.
10 *Ep. Carn.*, IV, Ch, 64; V, Hn, 36; Cn, 256; VI, Kp, 25; VIII, Tl, 200, 201, 206; Nr, 65, 69; Sb, 375; IX, Dv, 81; Dg, 23; XII, Mi, 83, Si, 95; Tp, 9; Tm, 11, 37; Pg, 69; *Ep. Ind.*, III, pp. 40, 124, 228; Butterworth, o. c., I, p. 112; *M. A. R.*, 1912-13, p. 43; 1916, p. 58, 59, 60; 1918, p. 50; 1925, p. 45, 100.
11 *Ep. Carn.*, III, Sr, 11, 15, V, 89; Ml, 121; 134; V, HN, 7; Hn, 3, 86, 133; Cn, 256; VII, Ci, 13; IX, Ht, 34; X, Bg, 70; Gd, 46; Ml, 158; XI, Dg, 34, 67; *Ep. Ind.*, VIII, p. 305; XVII, p. 202,
12 *Ep. Ind.*, XVIII, p. 144.

Saṅgamēśa [1], Saṅgamēśvara [2], Saṅgamēśvarat [3] and Saṅgama-nripēndra [4]. This name perhaps reveals his original native place Saṅgama. There was a village called Saṅgama in the Seringapatam Taluka. An inscription of 800 mentions one Prithuvi-gāmuṇḍa of Saṅgama as witness of a donation[5]. Several other villages with this name are found at the confluence of some rivers [6].

Saṅgama belonged to the Yādava race, as directly descending from Yādu [7]. He often, but not always, receives the title of 'king' in the inscriptions [8]. In a very few inscriptions, he appears as an obscure person, or at least one whose deeds were not worth recording but for his children. Thus Bukka I is called in a lithic record: "That moon to the ocean

[1] *Ep. Carn.*, X, Bg, 70.

[2] *Ep. Carn.*, V, Bl, 148; Hn, 36; *M. A. R.*, 1924, p. 36; 1925, p. 31.

[3] *Ep. Carn.*, IX, Nl, 53.

[4] *Ep. Carn.*, X, Kl, 64.

[5] *Ep. Carn.*, IV, Sr, 160.

[6] The city of Vijayanagara itself also was supposed to be next to the *Sangama* of two rivers. Harihara II is said to have made a grant "in the presence of the god Sri Virupakshadeva, at (the confluence of) the Tunga and the Bhadra" *J. B. B. R. A. S.*, XII, p. 377.

[7] *Ep. Carn.*, III, Ml, 121; Sr, 11, 15, 89; TN, 134; V, Cn, 256; Hn, 36, 86, 133; HN, 7; Bl, 148; VI, Kp, 25; VII, Ci, 13; VIII, Tl, 200, 201, 203; Nr, 65, 69; IX, Hk, 37; Dv, 81; X, Bg, 70; Ml, 158; Gd, 46; XI, Dg, 34; XII, Pg, 69; Tp, 9; Tm, 11, 37; Si, 95; *Ep. Ind.*, III, p. 40 and 124; XVII, p. 202 and 116; XVIII, p. 144; Butterworth, o. c., I, p. 14 and 112; *M. A. R.*, 1911-12, p. 49; 1912-13, p. 43; 1916, p. 58, 59 and 60; 1918, p. 50; 1924, p. 36; 1925, p. 31 and 100.

[8] *Ep. Carn.*, III, Sr, 11, 15; V, HN, 36, 86, 133; VI, Kp, 25; VII, Ci, 13; VIII, Sb, 375; Tl, 206; Ng, 65, 69; IX, Nl, 53; Hk, 34, X, Gd, 46; Ml, 158; XII, Tm, 37; Si, 95; Rice, *Mysore Inscriptions*, p. 279; *Ep. Ind.*, III, p. 124-5; XVII, p. 202 and 116; XVIII, p. 144; Butterworth, o. c., I, p. 14; *M. A. R.*, 1916, p. 58; 1925, p. 100.

Saṅgamēśa" [1]; and in another one he is said to be "a son on account of whom Saṅgama was famous" [2]. Nevertheless the majority of the inscriptions extol very highly the qualities of Saṅgama as well as his personal achievements. "Vishnu", we read in one, "formed the intention of being born in the Lunar line under the name of Saṅgama" [3]. In fact he is said to be a person of the "highest qualities" [4], or "with noble qualities and free from sin" [5], and accordingly "a moon to the ocean of the Yadu-vaṁśa" [6], or "an assemblage of good qualities, a moon in expanding the great sea of Yādu race" [7]. "Sri Saṁgama," reads another inscription, "adorned that lineage (the Yādava race) with his virtue, just as the glorious time of spring alone, with its bursting forth of blossoms, adorns the assemblage of the seasons" [8]. His devotion is expressly extolled: "At Ramēśvara and many other places abounding in various holy deeds, he, with joyful heart, surrounded by learned men repeatedly gave according to the rite the sixteen great gifts, thus redoubling his fame, which already manifest was sung by the inhabitants of the three worlds" [9]. And then playing with the meaning of the name Saṅgama, he is declared to be "a mine of good qualities and in whom was seen the rare union of the goddess of wealth and of learning" [10]. The same idea is expressed in different ways, as for instance: "Who was a union, the

---

[1] *Ep. Carn.*, X, Bg, 70.
[2] *Ep. Carn.*, IV, Ch, 64.
[3] *Ep. Carn.*, XI, Dg, 23.
[4] *Ep. Carn.*, VIII, Nr, 69.
[5] *M. A. R.*, 1925, p. 100.
[6] *Ep. Carn.*, V, Hn, 133.
[7] *M. A. R.*, 1925, p. 45.
[8] *J. B. B. R. A. S.*, XII, p. 372. Cf. Rice, *Mysore Inscriptions*, p. 55.
[9] *J. B. B. R. A. S.*, XII, p. 372.
[10] Ibid., p. 31.

most difficult to effect, of Śrī and Sarasvatī"[1], which seems not to be an empty boast; for we read in another inscription that in him "the goddesses of wealth and learning found a happy protector"[2], and another states that he was "well versed in all sciences"[3]. Other inscriptions praise him as a great warrior: "the breezes of the chāmaras (that fanned him)," says one, "being the long drawn sighs of the wives of his enemies"[4]. And another, referring to him, states the following: "The might of whose arm was sung everywhere, whom they here called indeed Kārtāvirya in valour, the Himālayas in courage, and the sun in splendour"[5] "King Saṅgama", we also read in a third one, "of good conduct, wearing Śaśimauli (Śiva) as an ornamental jewel: on whose victories in battles the crowds of enemy kings having burdened (with numbers) though vanquished reach the cardinal points in great haste; (but) whose (i. e. the King's) fame moves on (passing) through intervening spaces amidst lords of the eight directions"[6]. Another inscription says that his "uncontrolled high valour... overclouded the unchecked fighting power of hostile kings, whose shining excellent lotus-feet were worshipped by the great splendour of the rubies on the humbly bent heads of crores of princes"[7]. And as a consequence of his victories another lithic record commemorates that "he spread forth his commands, as if they were garlands on the heads of the rulers of the earth"[8].

Ep. Carn., V, Bl, 148.
M. A. R., 1924, p. 36.
Ep. Ind., XV, p. 24.
Ep. Carn., XI, Dv, 81.
Butterworth, o. c., I, p. 113.
Ep. Ind., XVIII, p. 202.
Ep. Ind., III, p. 32, V, 2.
J. B. B. R. A. S., XII, p. 372.

Again in another it is read: "This glorious lord Saṅgama, who was an auspicious mirror to the goddes of Heroes"[1]. Another inscription is more explicit as regards his campaigns: "He performed the 16 great gifts in Rāmēśvaram and other holy places. Quickly damming the Kāvēri when in full flood, he crossed over and seizing the enemy alive took possession of his Tancha kingdom (Tanjore), and of the city Śrīrangapaṭṭaṇa. He conquered Chēra, Chōḷa and Paṇḍya together with the lord of Madhurā, Manubhūsha, the Turushka and the Gajapati king"[2]. A new inscription speaks of his administrative qualities: "The glorious lord Saṅgama, by whom all subjects were protected according to ancient rules"[3]. All these heroic deeds and able administration are presupposed by some inscriptions that make the following statement about Saṅgama: "By whom the Lakshmī — the Karnaṭa-dēśa — was enabled permanently to wear her earrings"[4].

From the study of all these epigraphical extracts the following conclusions may be drawn:—

1. Saṅgama was a nobleman and a warrior.

2. He defeated several kings of Southern India and captured the city of Seringapatam.

3. He was a petty king most likely under the Hoysaḷas, who are not mentioned among Saṅgama's enemies.

4. The petty principality governed by Saṅgama was within the limits of Karnaṭaka.

[1] *Ep. Ind.*, III, p. 124.

[2] *M. A. R.*, 1918, p. 50. Cf. Ibid., p. 51, and *J. B. B. R. A. S.*, XII, p. 372-373.

[3] *Ep. Ind.*, III, p. 124-5.

[4] *Ep. Carn.*, VIII, Tl, 206; Nr. 69; XII, Pg, 69.

5. Most likely as a general of the Hoysaḷa army, Saṅgama waged war against the Mussulmans of northern India and against the Sultan of Madura, called by the inscription Manubhusha (..........Shah)[1].

5. THE ANCESTORS OF SANGAMA

These kingly qualities of Saṅgama seem to have been inherited from his father Bukka[2], "whose valour", says an inscription, "was difficult to rival"[3]. Sangama's mother is called Māyāmbikā[4], Māgāmbikā[5] and Megāmbikā[6]. According to the Hosahaḷḷi copper-plate grant of Harihara II the father of Saṅgama was named Anant[7]. We do not know anything else of this Bukka[8] or Anant, nor of his ancestors up to Yādu himself, except the isolated mention of one Janārdana, who is once referred to as one of the ancestors of Bukka I[9].

Nevertheless in the inscriptions of the Hoysaḷa Emperors we come across a noble family at the Hoysaḷa court, from which the family of Saṅgama seems to have descended,

---

1 Quite properly Mr. H. H. Wilson said that Bukka was the son of a neighbouring Raja. Cf. *Asiatic Researches*, XX, p. 6.

2 *Ep. Carn.*, X, Gd, 46; Ml, 150; Butterworth, o. c., I, p. 113.

3 Butterworth, l. c.

4 *Ep. Carn.*, X, Gd, 46.

5 *Ep. Carn.*, X, Ml, 158.

6 Butterworth, o. c., I, p. 113.

7 *J. B. H. S.*, I, p. 130.

8 Messrs. Butterworth and Venugopaul Chetty, with the preconceived idea that all the Vijayanagara Dynasties are Telugu, are inclined to identify Sangama's father with a chief named Bukkaraya Odayalu who receives several honorific titles in an inscription at the Nellore District. Cf. Butterworth, o. c., III, p. 1467. But the father of this Bukkaraya Odayalu seems to be a Reddi chief. Cf. Ibid., II, p. 643.

9 *M. A. R.*, 1916, p. 61. Mr. Venkayya vainly attempted to unite

(*To face p. 74*)

Geneological Tree of Kesiraja's Family

- Ramadaṇḍādhipa
  - Śrīdhara-daṇḍanātha
    - Mallidēva-daṇḍādhipa *or* Malla-chamūpa
      - Mādhava
      - Beṭṭarasa (m. to Lakshmi)
        - Harihara-dēva
        - Mādhava-chamūpa
        - Āchaṇa-dāṇḍanātha
        - Dāvarasa
        - Kēśava-daṇḍanātha *or* Kēśirāja-chamūpati *or* Kēsava-chamunātha (m. to Padmāva)
          - Balla *or* Vallala-daṇḍēśa
          - Mādhava
          - Beṭṭasēnāni
        - Mallapa (m. to Nāgala-dēvi)
          - Dāvana-daṇḍanātha
          - Kēśava-dēva
          - Beṭṭa-chamūpa
        - Māramayya
        - Kañchla-dēvi
      - Dama-ḍāṇḍēśa
    - Dāma-rāja
    - Kēśava Rāja

The annexed table is the pedigree of this family according to the genealogy given in the inscription.

The reasons that seem to suggest the identification of this family with the ancestors of the first Vijayanagara Dynasty are the following:—

1. This is the only Yādava family found in the inscriptions besides the ruling family of the Hoysaḷas. Thus, the minister Kēśava-chamunātha is said to be "born in the Yādu-vaṁśa" [1].

2. This family is as old as the Hoysaḷa family itself, for, as the inscription reads, "when the Poysaḷa (Hoysaḷa) line began, then Kēśirāja's line began" [2].

3. Consequently they are the most prominent noble family under the Hoysaḷas. Hence the same inscription concludes: "Can those new generals whose line began but yesterday be compared with him?" [3].

4. For several generations the members of this family were ministers or generals of the Hoysaḷa Emperors:

(a) "Vinayāditya's councillor was the celebrated Ramadaṇḍādhipa".

(b) "Śrīdhara-daṇḍanātha was king Ereyaṅga's favourite minister".

(c) "Śrīdhara's sons, the lord Malidēva-daṇḍādhipa, the chief councillor Dāma-rāja, and the chief general Kēśava

the Sangama family with the Yadavas of Devgiri. Cf. *Ind. Ant.*, XV, p. 12. Mr. Suryanarain Rao, *The Never To Be Forgotten Empire*, p. 163-4, refers to an inscription of the year 1295 mentioning one Bukkana Odeyar and his father Hukkana Odeyar, whom he supposes to be some of the ancestors of Sangama. Sorry we cannot form our opinion as regards this inscription, for the 4 references given by Mr. Suryanarain to *Ep. Carn.*, V, are all wrong.

[1] *Ep. Carn.*, V, Cn, 244. [2] Ibid. [3] Ibid.

Rāja were the three chief promoters of Vishnuvardhana's kingdom".

(d) "Mallachamūpa's three sons, the minister Mādhava, the minister Beṭṭarasa and Dāma-daṇḍēśa were ministers who subdued the enemies of king Nārasiṁha and freed all the land from them".

(e) Speaking of the seven sons and one daughter of Beṭṭarasa the inscription reads: "In king Ballaḷa (II)'s kingdom they were all distinguished for the highest merit, valour and learning"

(f) Kēśirāja is called "King-Ballaḷa (II)'s great minister, a rampart to his ruler's extensive dominions"..."He constructed a large tank, granted a great agrāhara and built a temple surmounted with a golden kalaśa. In Nallūr and Taḷirūr, in Bāgiyūr and Bālgarchche and in the celebrated Beḷgali did Kēśirāja's works of charity shine. In Beḷgali he made splendid tanks and a temple. The groves he planted, the tank he built, and the line of temples, attract the eye in the agrāhara that he granted...What all the generals said was as if written in water, what the general Kēśava said was alone as if written on stone, in king Ballaḷa's council".

(g) One of the sons of Kēśava, Mādhava, is called 'minister': while the three sons of Mallapa are also styled 'the King's chief ministers'.

5. This family, just as the family of Sangama, is called a "Karṅata family".

6. Finally several names of the members of this family, such as Mādhava, Harihara, Dēvarāsa, Mallapa, are also names of the family of Saṅgama, and we see them repeated in several generations.

It is not improbable therefore that the ancestors of the first dynasty of Vijayanagara were the members of the famous family of Kēśavadaṇḍanātha.

Yet where was the family of Saṅgama settled before his sons were called to occupy such important posts in the Hoysala Empire? No satisfactory reply to this question has been given hitherto. Anyhow there is an inscription that gives a clue to ascertain the original settlement of Saṅgama and his sons. This inscription found in the Sorab Taluka informs us that Mārapa the fourth son of Saṅgama "from Kallāsa acquired a kingdom in the West"[1], *viz.* Chandragutti. It seems therefore that before the appointment of Mārapa as governor of Chandragutti, he was residing at Kalasa. Was the whole family of Saṅgama settled at this ancient capital? The fact that Harihara I and his brothers in 1346 and then Bukka I alone paid visits to the math of Śringeri, not far from Kalāsa, suggests some family connection with that neighbourhood. On the other hand the king of Kalāsa contemporary of Ballala III, in 1296, was one Paṇḍya Dēva[2] of the Paṇḍyas of Uchchangi. These Paṇḍyas also belonged to the Yādava race[3]. All these details seem to point to Kalasa or its surroundings as the place where Saṅgama and his sons were settled, before the foundation of Vijayanagara[4]. Now about 15 miles north east of Kalasa at the place where the river Bhadra is joined by the Anebidda-halla there is the town of Sangamēśvara[5]. Was this perhaps the birth place of Harihara's and Bukka's father[6]?

1 *Ep. Carn.*, VIII, Sb, 375. 2 *Ep. Carn.*, VI, Cm, 36.

3 *Ep. Carn.*, XI, p. 18.

4 A much damaged inscription at Coorg of the year 1297 mentions one Harihara with the title of mahamandalesvara. Could it be possible that Harihara I occupied a similar post in the south-west corner of the Hoysala Empire, before being entrusted with the defence of the northern frontier. Cf. *Ep. Carn.*, I, Cg, 59.

5 Cf. Rice, *Mysore*, II, p. 432.

6 If the Sangama family's place of origin was the District of Kadur, as the above reasons seem to point out, could the fact that Sosavur, the original place of the Hoysalas, is in the same western corner of that district be a mere coincidence?

6. RELATIONSHIP BETWEEN THE HOYSALAS AND THE FIRST VIJAYANAGARA DYNASTY.

We have already seen that the family of Saṅgama was most likely, and if identified with the family of Kēśirāja without any doubt, subordinate to the Hoysaḷa Emperors. Was there any relationship between the two families?

First of all the Hoysaḷas belonged to the Lunar race and to the Yādava family, as well as the members of the first Vijayanagara Dynasty [1]. All the members of the Hoysaḷa Dynasty receive in the inscriptions pompous titles declaring their descent from Yādu. All these titles are collected in the following table:-

Hoysala Kings	Yadava Title	Inscription
Saḷa	The ornament of that Yādava race	*Ep. Carn.*, IV, Mg, 38.
	An ornament of the Yādu-vaṁśa	*Ep. Carn.*, VI, Cm, 20.
	A head-jewel of Yādava kings	*Ep. Carn.*, VI, Cm, 137.
Kāma Hoysaḷa	Sun in the sky of the Yādava-kula	*Ep. Carn.*, V, Ak, 141, 142.

[1] *Ep. Carn.*, III, TN, 97; Md, 121; IV, Kr, 9, 10, 63; Ng, 29, 30, 32, 38, 98; V, Ak, 62, 71, 118; Bl, 9, 16, 58, 74, 86, 92, 112, 124, 171, 193, 224; Hn, 61, 65, 84, 85, 116, 119; Cn, 224, 236, 238; VI, Tk, 61, 87, 88; Cm, 21, 22, 78, 137; Kd, 4, 16, 51, 67, 79, 95, 129, 148, 156; VII, Sk, 138, 235; Ci, 52; VIII, Sb, 28; XI, Cd, 32; Dg, 25; XII, Tp, 42; 54, 123 bis; Kg, 1; *M. A. R.*, 1923, p. 39.

Hoysala Kings	Yadava Title	Inscription
Vinayāditya	Sun in the Yādava sky	*Ep. Carn.*, VI, Kd, 22, 30.
	Sun in the sky of the Yādava-kula	*Ep. Carn.*, IV, Kr, 49.
		Ep. Carn., V, Bl, 200.
		Ep. Carn., VI, Cm, 160.
	The sun of the ornament of the Yādava-kula	*Ep. Carn.*, IV, Ng, 28.
	The sun in the eastern mountains, the Yādava-kula	*Ep. Carn.*, V, Bl, 119.
	A branch of the tree of plenty, the Yādu-vaṁśa	*Ep. Carn.*, V, Ak, 93.
Ballaḷa I	The king of the Yādavas	*Ep. Carn.*, V, Ak, 74.
	The upraiser of the Yādu-vaṁśa	*Ep. Carn.*, V, Ak, 48.
		Ep. Carn., V, Hn, 65.
	Sun in the sky of the Yādava-kula	*Ep. Carn.*, IV, Kr, 55.
		Ep. Carn., V, Bl, 141.

Hoysala Kings	Yadava Title	Inscription
		Ep. Carn., VI, Kd, 2.
Ballaḷa I	The sun in the sky of the Yādava-kula	*Ep. Carn.*, V, Bl, 199.
	A sun in the sky of the Yādava family	*Ep. Carn.*, X, Bp, 10.
	An ornament of the Yādu-kula	*Ep. Carn.*, V, Bl, 2.
Vishnuvardhana	The Yādu Rāja	*Ep. Carn.*, XII, Gb, 13.
	Tha Yādava Narayana	*Ep. Carn.*, VI, Kd, 96.
	The Yādava lion	*Ep. Carn.*, XII, Kg, 1.
	The ornament of the Yādus	*Ep. Carn.*, V, Cn, 149.
	The ornament of the Yādu-kula	Ibid.
	Promoter of the Yādu-vaṁśa	*Ep. Carn.*, V, Bl, 58.
	The promoter of the Yādu-vaṁśa	*Ep. Carn.*, IV, Ng, 30.
		Ep. Carn., V, Cn, 186.
		Ep. Carn., V, Bl, 71, 77, 117, 147.

Hoysala Kings	Yadava Title	Inscription
		Ep, Carn., VI, Kd, 117, 127, 148, 156.
Vishnuvardhana	The promoter of the Yādu-vaṁśa	*Ep. Carn.*, VI, Tk, 61.
		Ep. Carn., XII, Tp. 128.
		Ep. Carn., XII, Gb, 13.
	The up-raiser of the Yādu-vaṁśa	*Ep. Carn.*, V, Ak, 43.
	The sun to the Yādu-kula	*Ep. Carn.*, V, Cn, 145.
	Sun in the sky of the Yādavas	*Ep. Carn.*, V, Hn, 114.
	Sun in the sky of the Yādava-kula	*Ep. Carn.*, V, Ak, 52.
		Ep. Carn., V, Hn, 130.
		Ep. Carn., XII, Tp, 58.
	Sun in the sky of the Yādu-kula	*Ep. Carn.*, XII, Tm, 9.
	Sun in the sky of the Yādava race	*Ep. Carn.*, IV, Ch, 83, 98.

Hoysala Kings	Yadava Title	Inscription
Vishnuvardhana	Sun in the sky of the Yādava line	*Ep. Carn.*, IV, Gu, 69.
	A golden finial to the royal palace, the Yādava race	*Ep. Carn.*, III, Sr, 49.
	The crowning ornament of the Yādu-kula	*Ep. Carn.*, IV, Ng, 3.
	Foundation pillar of the palace of kingly merit which caused the Yādava-kula to ripen	*Ep. Carn.*, XII, Gb, 13.
Udayāna *or* Udayāditya	A full moon in raising the waters of the ocean the kingdom of the Yādava kings	*Ep. Carn.*, V, Bl, 17.
Narasimha I	The Yādava Narayana	*Ep. Carn.*, V, Hn, 69.
		Ep. Carn., Cn, 221.
		Ep. Carn., XI, Dg, 137.
	The Yādava chakravarti	*Ep. Carn.*, V, Ak, 151.
		Ep. Carn., XI, Cd, 23.

Hoysala Kings	Yadava Title	Inscription
Narasiṁha I	The Yādu chief of the world	*Ep. Carn.*, VII, Sk, 105.
	The ornament of the Yādava-kula	*Ep. Carn.*, VII, Sk, 186.
	The ornament of the Yādu race	*Ep. Carn.*, III Sr, 74.
	The glory of the Yādu-kula	*Ep. Carn.*, V, Cn, 197.
	Sun in the sky of the Yādava-kula	*Ep. Carn.*, III, TN, 86.
		Ep. Carn., V, Ak, 52.
		Ep. Carn., XII, Tm, 38.
	Sun in the sky of the Yādava race	*Ep. Carn.*, IV, Ch, 13.
	Moon to the water-lily, the Yādu-kula	*Ep. Carn.*, V, Hn, 69.
Ballaḷa II	The Yādu king	*Ep. Carn.*, V, Cn, 172.
		Ep. Carn., V, Bl, 112.
	The generous Yādava Emperor	*Ep. Carn.*, V, Bl, 136.
	The Yādava Narayana	*Ep. Carn.*, V, Bl, 129.

Hoysala Kings	Yadava Title	
		Ep. Carn., VI, Kd, 117.
		Ep. Carn., VII, Sk, 196, 247.
		Ep.Carn., VIII, Sb, 4, 171, 377, 378, 514, 516.
		Ep. Carn., XI, Cd, 23.
		Ep. Carn., XI, Hk, 4, 13.
		M.A.R., 1912-13, p. 40.
Ballala II	The Yādava chakravarti	*Ep. Carn.*, V, Ak, 154.
		Ep. Carn., VII, Sk, 145, 148, 156, 168, 173, 244.
		Ep.Carn., VIII, Sb, 307.
	The Hoysaṇa Yādava-chakravarti	*Ep.Carn.*, VIII, Sb, 305.
	An ornament of the Yādu-kula	*Ep. Carn.*, V, Bl, 2.
	Glory of the Yādava-kula	*Ep. Carn.*, VII, Sk, 105.
	Sun in the Yādava sky	*Ep. Carn.*, V, Hn, 31.
	Sun in the sky of the Yādava-kula	*Ep. Carn.*, I, p. 72.

Hoysala Kings	Yadava Title	Inscription
		Ep. Carn., VI, Kd, 117.
	Sun in the sky of the Yādava race	*Ep. Carn.*, IV, Ng, 29.
Narasiṁha II	Sun in the sky of the Yādava kula	*Ep. Carn.*, III, Md, 121
Somēśvara *or* Siṁhana	Yādava Raya	*Ep.Carn.*, VIII, Sb, 275.
	The Yādava Narayana	*Ep. Carn.*, VII, Sk, 248, 268, 270.
		Ep. Carn., VII Hl, 20.
		Ep. Carn., VIII, Sb, 217, 250, 269, 231, 339, 387, 398, 403, 423, 425.
	The Yādava-Chakravarti	*Ep. Carn.*, VII, Sk, 243.
		Ep.Carn., VIII, Sb, 256, 308.
	Sun in the sky of the Yādava-kula	*Ep. Carn.*, VI, Cm, 1.
		Ep.Carn., VIII, Sr, 14.
		Ep.Carn., VIII, Sb. 492.

Hoysala Kings	Yadava Title	Inscription
Somēsvara	A sun in causing the lotus, the Yādava-kula, to unfold	*Ep. Carn.*, VII, Sk, 95. *Ep.Carn.*, VIII, Sb. 276.
	Sun in causing to unfold the lotus, the Yādava-kula	*Ep.Carn.*, VIII, Sb, 391.
Narasiṁha III	The Yādu Rāja	*Ep. Carn.*, XII, Gb, 30.
	The Yādava chakravarti	*Ep. Carn.*, V, Ak, 151.
	Sun in the sky of the Yādava-kula	*Ep. Carn.*, XII Tp, 2. *Ep. Carn.*, XII, Tm, 49.
Rāmanatha *or* Rāmachandra *or* Rāmadeva	The Yādava Narayana	*Ep. Carn.*, VII, Sk, 122, 141, 172, 203, 211. *Ep. Carn.*, VII, Ci, 2, 23. *Ep. Carn.*, VII, Hl, 12, 17, 18, 29. *Ep.Carn.*, VIII, Sb, 31, 57, 101, 128, 160, 189, 198, 208. 219. 247.

Hoysala Kings	Yadava Title	Inscription
		275, 284, 292, 352, 507.
Rāmanatha	The Yādava Narayana	*Ep. Carn.*, VIII, Sr, 86.
		Ep. Carn., XI. Dg, 81.
	The Yādava-chakravarti	*Ep. Carn.*, VII, Sk, 140.
	A Sun in causing to unfold the lotus the Yādava-kula	*Ep. Carn.*, VII, Hl, 17.
Ballala III	Sun in the Yādava sky	*Ep, Carn.*, V. Hn, 31.
		Ep. Carn., XI, Cd, 1.
	Sun in the sky of the Yādava-kula	*Ep. Carn.*, III, Ml, 14.
		Ep. Carn., IX, Bn, 34.
		Ep. Carn., IX, Cp, 123.
	Sun in the sky of the Yādava family	*Ep. Carn.*, IX, Hk, 134.
		M.A.R., 1913-14, p. 44.
	A sun in the sky of the Yādava family	*Ep. Carn.*, X, Bp. 10.

From the perusal of the above table it is not difficult to conclude that the Hoysaḷa Emperors were supposed to be the supreme representatives of the Yādava race in Southern India. Indeed the head of the Hoysaḷa family, king Saḷa[1],—who was king of the region in which the Tuṅgabhadrā is born [2]—"became Poysaḷa by killing the tiger in Śaśakapura, and from him arose the Poysaḷa-vaṁśa" [3]. All the inscriptions refer to this event as the starting point of the Hoysaḷa family[4]. By this heroic act Saḷa "acquired the name Poysaḷa as a family name" [5]; hence all his descendants "acquired the name of Hoysaḷa, as the Yādavas from Yādu" [6], and consequently "from which time forth that name of Poysaḷa was the designation of the Yādu Kings" [7].

But the inscriptions suggest something more important. Not only the descendents of Saḷa became Hoysaḷas; but "that name (Hoysaḷa) was acquired by the Yādava-kula"[8]. "Thenceforward the Yādu-vaṁśa was known as the Poysaḷa-vaṁśa" [9], says another inscription; and a third one states: "whence the Yādava race from that time obtained the name Hoysaḷa" [10].

These general statements evidently refer to the Yāda-

[1] *Ep. Carn.*, V, Bl, 125.
[2] *Ep. Carn.*, VII, 235.
[3] *Ep. Carn.*, V, Ak, 183.
[4] *Ep. Carn.*, III, Md, 121. Cf. *Ep. Carn.*, VI, Kd, 12a, 129, 136, 143, 148, 156; Tk, 61; XI, Dg, 25; XII, Tp, 42.
[5] *Ep. Carn.*, VI, Kd, 51.
[6] *Ep. Carn.*, V, Bl, 74. Cf. *Ep. Carn .*, V, Hn, 61; VI, Kd, 4; VII, Sk, 138, 235.
[7] *Ep. Carn.*, VI, Cm, 20. Cf. *Ep. Carn.*, V, Ak, 71; Bl, 124.
[8] *Ep. Carn.*, V, Ak, 180.
[9] *Ep. Carn.*, V, Bl, 171. Cf. *Ep Carn.*, V, Hn, 65.
[10] *Ep. Carn.*, V, Bl, 86.

vas settled in Southern India within the boundaries of the Hoysaḷa Empire. Now, the fact that all the Yādavas in this territory are said to have adopted the surname of Hoysaḷas is confirmed by another inscription: the one that speaks of the great minister Kēśava-daṇḍanatha and his family, that belonged to the Yādu-vaṁśa. Nevertheless they professed to be Hoysaḷas, as the inscription tells us: "When the Poysaḷa line began, then Kēśirāja's line began"[1]. And another inscription, of the time of Ballāḷa II corroborates this conclusion: "From the tree of plenty, the Yadu-vaṁśa", says this record, "sprang many as branches in the Hoysaḷānvaya, distinguished among whom was born Vinayāditya"[2]. It is therefore an incontrovertible fact that there were many Hoysaḷa branches in Southern India, as early as the time of Vinayāditya, apparently the grandson of Saḷa.

This evidently means either that all the Yādavas of the southern territories were of the family of Saḷa, though not all perhaps directly descended from him; or that all the Yādavas living in that kingdom adopted the glorious name of Hoysaḷa, made so famous, as the surname of the ruling family belonging to their own Kula. In any case the family of Saṅgama, who had settled in Karṇataka, most likely as feudatory to the Hoysaḷas, and probably was descended from the family of Kēśirāja, also adopted the surname of Hoysaḷa.

But was this family in any way connected with the imperial Hoysaḷas ? A phrase in the account of Ferishta seems to refer to this family connection. It is there related that in order to save his kingdom from any further invasion by the northern Muhammadans, "Bilal Dew (Ballāḷa Dēva) convened a meeting of his kinsmen, and resolved, first, to se-

---

[1] *Ep. Carn.*, V, Cn, 244.
[2] *Ep. Carn.*, XII, Tp, 123 bis.

cure the forts of his own country" [1]. The fortification of Vīra-Vijaya-Virūpākshapura in the northern frontier and the appointment of Harihara, as his mahāmandalēśvara in the renewed city, were two of the practical results of that meeting. Hence it seems quite natural that this mahāmandalēśvra Harihara, to whom the most responsible post in the Empire was entrusted on that occasion, should be one of those kinsman of Ballāḷa III convened by him to prepare the defence of his Empire. In fact other relations of the Hoysaḷa Emperor were placed in command of other forts and provinces of not so great importance. Thus his Alija (son-in-law) Gaṅji-Dēva-daṇṇāyaka, in the year 1333 "was in the residence of Penugoṇde (Penukonda), ruling the kingdom in peace and wisdom"[2]. Similarly Sōmeya Daṇṇāyaka, Ballāḷa's brother-in-law "governed Emmatūra-durga (Chitaldroog)," in the year 1333 [3].

And indeed from the study of the Mysore inscriptions it is evident that such relationship between Ballāḷa III and Harihara did really exist. One of the officers of Ballāḷa III was Dādiya Sōmaya [4] mentioned a little while before. He was also called Dādi Sōmaya dannāyaka [5], Dādi Sōmeya-dannāyaka [6], Pādiya (Dadiya)— daṇṇāyaka [7], or simply Sōmarasa[8]. He is once given the Tamilized form of Dātiya Sōmaiya-daṇṇāyakkar [9]. He receives the following titles: Mahaman-

---

[1] Ferishta-Briggs, I, p. 427.
[2] *M. A. R.*, 1912-13, p. 40.
[3] *Ep. Carn.*, X, Gd, 16.
[4] *Ep. Carn.*, IX, Hk, 43.
[5] *Ep. Carn.*, IX, Hk. 75.
[6] *Ep. Carn.*, IX, Kn, 69; *M. A. R.*, 1911-12, p. 45; 1912-13, p. 40.
[7] *Ep. Carn.*, VI, Cm, 105.
[8] *Ep. Carn.*, IX, Cp, 73.
[9] *Ep. Carn.*, X, An, 84.

dalēśvara [1], great minister [2] the king's house minister [3], and chief minister [4], and king [5]. His office of Daṇṇāyaka together with all these titles evidently prove that Dādiya Sōmaya was a Kshatriya. His name Sōmaya likewise discloses that he belonged to the Lunar race [6]. And his family alliance with the families of Ballāḷa III and Harihara will readily convince anybody that Dādiya Sōmaya was a member of the Yādava-kula. And indeed this minister of Ballāḷa III, who also employed Sōmaya's sons as his ministers and generals, seems to be the descendant of Kēśirāja, in whose family, as seen above, the hereditary office of minister had already remained for several generations.

Sōmaya Daṇṇāyaka who had been in charge of the government of Bemmatūra-durga (Chitaldroog) [7], was married to a sister of Ballaḷa III, whose name is not given [8]. The eldest son of this union was Siṅgeya-danāyaka or Śiṇgedaṇṇāyakkar [9]. This Siṅgeya is called "great minister" of Ballāla III from 1318 to 1343[10], though he seems to be related to the king from earlier times [11]. He is once called a son (nephew) of Ballāḷa III [12]. The second son of Sōmaya,

[1] *Ep. Carn.*, IX, Cp, 73.
[2] *Ep. Carn.*, VI, Cm, 105; IX, Kn, 69.
[3] *Ep. Carn.*, IV, Cn, 73.
[4] *Ep. Carn.*, IX, Hk, 75.
[5] *Ep. Carn.*, IX, Hk. 43.
[6] Some may say that Somaya or Soma was an abreviation of Somashekara. After considering all the circumstances of this case, this surmise does not seem probable.
[7] *M. A. R.*, 1911-12, p. 45.
[8] *M. A. R.*, 1912-13, p. 40.
[9] *M. A. R.*, 1912-13, p. 41; *Ep. Carn.*, IX, An, 84; IX, Hk, 90.
[10] *Ep. Carn.*, IX, Hk, 140, 140a; Cn, 10, 31; X, Bp, 63; Mr, 16.
[11] *Ep. Carn.*, IX, An, 80.
[12] *Ep. Carn.*, IX, Hk, 104.

and consequently younger brother of Siṅgeya, was Vallapa or Ballapa daṇṇāyaka or daṇṇāyakar (in the Tamil inscriptions)[1]. In the year 1342 he is called "the great minister in the palace of Poysaḷa-śrī-vīra Vallāla-Devar"[2]; and he seems to have accompanied the Emperor in his war against the Sultan of Madura, for in the following year 1343 a grant was made "for the success of the sword and arm of Vallappa-deṇṇāyakkar"[3]. He is also called "the son (nephew) of the Pratapa-chakravarti Pośaḷa vīra Vallāḷa Devar"[4].

This Vallapa-daṇṇāyaka, the son of the great minister of Ballaḷa III, who became the great minister in the palace of the said Emperor, whose nephew he was on his mother's side, had married a daughter of Harihara I, as he is called Harihara I's Aliya[5]; and from this marriage we know of a son named Tanan[6]. When was this marriage celebrated, before or after the death of Ballāḷa? The age of Vallappa, who one year before Ballāḷa's death is already called the great minister in the latter's palace, seems to suggest a marriage earlier than this date. There is besides the fact that in 1339, when Ballāḷa III was in his residence at Vīra-Vijaga-Virūpākshapura, there was also there with him "the minister descended from that king Dādiya Sōmaya"[7]. Who was this minister, the son of Dādiya Sōmaya, residing at Vijayanagara together with the Emperor Ballāḷa III? Unfortunately this inscription is much worn out and the

1 *Ep. Carn.*, VI, Cm, 105; IX, Hk, 49, 90, 96; X, Bp, 10; Mr, 10, 12, 16, 18, 28.
2 *Ep. Carn.*, IX, Hk, 90.
3 *Ep. Carn.*, X, Mr, 16.
4 Ibid., 10, 12, 16, 18. Cf. *Ep. Carn.*, IX, Hk, 96.
5 *Ep. Carn.*, VI, Sg, 1; *M. A. R.*, 1916, p. 57.
6 *Ep. Carn.*, X, Mr, 18.
7 *Ep. Carn.*, IX, Hk, 43.

name of the minister is not readable. Yet it will not be a totally ungrounded assertion if we suppose that Vallappa, who was the great minister of Ballāḷa III 's palace, accompanied the sovereign on this occasion, in his visit to Vijayanagara and to his father-in-law, the new mahāmaṇḍalēśvara of the old kingdom of Hampe-Hastināvati. Twenty-two years later, in 1361, we find the same Vallapa-deṇṇayakar, acknowledging the authority of "the mahāmandalēśwara, the champion over kings who break their word, Ariyappa-udaiyar" his father-in-law [1].

All these facts undoubtedly disclose that the three families of Ballaḷa III, of Harihara I and of Dādiya Sōmaya, who so freely intermingled with one another, were not only Yādavas but also belonged to the same common stock of the Hoysaḷa-vaṁśa.

7. THE BROTHERS OF HARIHARA I

According to several inscriptions Saṅgama had only one son, Bukka [2]; he was in fact the one through whom the line of Saṅgama's family continued on the Vijayanagara throne. This is the reason why his brothers, and even Harihara I himself, are totally overlooked. Other inscriptions mentioned two sons, *viz.* Harihara and Bukka [3], both having ruled at Vijayanagara. One inscription mentions four sons of Saṅgama: Harihara, Śankara (?), Bukka and Marap-

---

[1] *Ep. Carn.*, IX, Bn, 101.

[2] *Ep. Carn.*, V, Bl, 148; Hn, 86, 133; VIII, Nr, 65; Tl, 200; IX, Dv, 81; XII, Si, 95; Tm, 11, 37; Pg, 69; *M. A. R.*, 1912-13, p. 43; 1916, p. 58, 59 and 60; 1924, 36; 1925, p. 100; *J. B. B. R. A. S.*, XII, p. 349. One inscription, *Ep. Carn.*, X, Cp, 34, gives Darkamahipala as the name of the only son of Sangama.

[3] *Ep. Carn.*, XI, Dg, 34; *J. B. B. R. A. S.*, XII, p. 373. Another inscription in *M. A. R.*, 1925, p. 31, mentions two sons of Sangama called Bukka and Bukka Raya.

pa[1]. Another records that he had five sons from his wife Śāradā, but two names only are given, Haryapa and Bukka[2]. Nevertheless the majority of the inscriptions refer to five brothers named Harihara, Kampa, Bukka, Māra or Mārapa and Mudda, Muddana or Muddapa[3]. These names are always given in the same order; hence it seems quite obvious that they are put in chronological succession, Harihara being the eldest and Muddapa being the youngest of the five. The position of Harihara during the last years of Vīra Ballāḷa III has been discussed at length in the previous pages. What was the occupation of his brothers is to be seen at present.

Kampa, under the name of Kampaṇati Oḍayar, is said in an inscription of the year 1346-7 to be "the lord of the eastern and western seas"[4]. This vague phrase is to be elucidated by the fact that this inscription is found in the village of Kodavalūru, Nellore District. Hence it is evident that Kampa ruled over at least a portion of the Telugu country in the East. All the inscriptions which we are going to refer to confirm this conclusion. Among them the Bitragunta inscription of Saṅgama II states that this Saṅgama succeeded his father in the government of the country; and from the places mentioned in the inscription it is clear that Saṅgama held some portions of the Nellore and Cuddapah Districts[5]. The government of the Nellore District, with the fortified hill of Udayagiri within its jurisdiction, was a very import-

---

1 *Ep. Carn.*, VIII, Sb, 375.

2 *Ep. Carn.*, V, Bl, 3.

3 *Ep. Carn.*, III, TN, 134; V, HN, 7; VII, Ci, 13; X, Gd, 46; Mb, 158; Bg, 70; XII, Tp, 9; *Ep. Ind.*, III, p. 32; Butterworth, I, p. 113; *M. A. R.*, 1916, p. 59.

4 Butterworth, II, p. 789-790.

5 *Ep. Ind.*, III, p. 32 and 34.

ant post as regards strategy in Southern India. Later on, Udayagiri was to be called "the chief fortress under the royal throne of Vijayanagara" [1]. The importance of this post was then specially relevant when the Mussulmans from Delhi had shortly before captured the city of Warangal, the capital of the Kākatīya Dynasty, just to the north of Udayagiri. The Nellore District was in fact the only way for the Afghan army to invade the south along the eastern coast. And it was precisely on this occasion, not long after the conquest of Warangal, that "Krishn Naig (Krishna Nāyaka), the son of Luddur Dew (Rudra Dēva), who lived near Wurungole (Warangal), went privately to Bilal Dew (Ballāḷa Dēva), Raja of Carnatic, and told him that he had heard the Mahomedans, who were now very numerous in the Deccan, had formed the design of extirpating all the Hindus, and that it was, therefore, advisable to combine against them" [2]. As a result of this information Ballāḷa III "convened a meeting of his kinsmen, and resolved, first, to secure the forts of his own country, and then to remove his seat of government among the mountains" [3]. Kampa therefore was placed in that responsible post by the same Vīra Ballāḷa, just as Harihara had been stationed at the new city Virūpākshapura in the centre of the northern frontier. That both the brothers ruled at the same time, one in the old Hastināvati kingdom and the other in the region of Udayagiri, is evident from the Bitragunta grant of Sangama II. After mentioning the five sons of Sangama, this document continues as follows: "Of these king Harihara, —by whom the Sultan, who resembled Indra, was defeated,—ruled the earth for a long

[1] *M. A. R.*, 1920, p. 39.
[2] Ferishta-Briggs, I, p. 427.
[3] Ibid.

time. His younger brother, king Kampana, whose name became true to its meaning, as he made the enemies tremble, ruled the earth for a long time" [1]. This passage shows that Harihara and Kampana ruled both simultaneously and friendly, as both are said to have ruled 'for a long time', and the second is not said to have succeeded the first. Moreover the fact that Saṅgama II, the son of Kampana, mentions in his grant his uncle Harihara, evidently discloses that Harihara and Kampana were in friendly terms. Yet one fails to see any sign of Kampa's succession after Harihara, as Mr. Krishna Sastri asserts [2]. Both brothers seem to have ruled at the same time and with the same authority, and in their respective dominions, independent of each other, at least during the life of the last Ballāḷas. In fact both seem to have died almost at the same time. For Bukka I is not found ruling over Vijayanagara till the year 1354 [3], and Kampana most likely died in the following year 1355 [4]. Yet he is also said to have ruled for a long time. Hence we cannot say that Kampana succeeded Harihara.

There is still another fact in connection with the rule of Kampana in the eastern districts that proves once more the intimate connection of the sons of Saṅgama with, and their subjection to Ballāḷa III. An inscription of the year 1343 found at Tēkal, Malur Taluka, Kolar District, records a grant of land to a temple "by the great minister Śōmappa, who was the protector of the kingdom of the mahāmaṇḍalēśwara, destroyer of hostile kings, champion over kings who break their word, Śrī-vīra-Kampaṇṇa Uḍaiyar" [5]. Three things

---

1. *Ep. Ind.*, III, p. 32.
2. Ibid., p. 24.
3. *Ep. Carn.*, XI, Cd, 2 and 3.
4. Cf. *Ep. Ind.*, III, p. 23.
5. *M. A. R.*, 1913-14, p. 46.

are to be noted in this passage: first of all the birūdas given to Kampa are the same as those given to his brothers Harihara and Bukka; showing therefore that he was also a dependent monarch just as they were. Then the place where the inscription is found proves that the jurisdiction of Kampa extended to a portion of the present District of Kolar, in the Mysore State. Finally, who was this minister Śōmappa is to be diligently investigated. He cannot be the great minister Dādiya Sōmaya-daṇṇāyaka, for his eldest son Siṅgeya is already called great minister of Ballāḷa III in 1318[1]. Hence the minister of Kampana, one year only after the death of Ballāḷa, must be a younger person. As a matter of fact an inscription of the year 1316 mentions one Vīra Sōmapa-Daṇṇāyaka, who is said to be the son of the same Vīra Ballāḷa III [2]. What was this relationship is not clear; he was perhaps the real son of Ballāḷa, but we are inclined to believe that he was a third son of Dādiya Sōmaya and hence nephew of Ballāḷa by the latter's sister. In any case the fact that so close a relative of the Hoysaḷa Emperor was acting as the minister of Kampa proves once more the intercourse between the Hoysaḷas and the Saṅgama familly, and even the relationship between both of them.

Three years after, in 1346, one Mudra chiddi Sāyanna Oḍayalu is mentioned as "the prime minister (mahāpradhāni) of Kanpanati Oḍayar" [3], in an inscription at Kodavalūru, Nellore District. Again a dateless charitable inscription at the same place is said to have been "engraved by Poddarāsu under the order of Sāyānna Oḍayalu" [4]. This Sāyana was the half brother of Mādhava Vidyāraṇya, who according to the colophon of his own work *Madhavīyā Dhātuvritti*, was "the

[1] Cf. supra. [2] *Ep Carn.*, IX, Kl, p. 104.
[3] Butterworth, II, p. 789. [4] Ibid., p. 791.

great minister of Samgamarāja, the son of Kamparāja, the glorious lord of the eastern, western and southern oceans"[1]. Their third brother Bhōginatha was the composer of the Bitragunta inscription and calls himself "the court jester of the king Samgama"[2]. Sāyanna continued ruling Nellore as late as the year 1364-5; for an inscription of this date at the city of Nellore still states that "Srīman Mahāmaṇḍalēśvara Vīra Śrī Sāvaṇṇa (Sāyaṇṇa) Oḍayalu was ruling the earth[3]". In this record nothing is said of Saṅgama. Accordingly one may rightly suspect that he had disappeared from the scene, as we do not hear of him any more, and that Sāyana continued ruling the Telugu province of the east on behalf of Bukka I, who already had at this time consolidated his power as an independent monarch, though he never assumed imperial titles. An inscription of 1380 mentions one Bāllapa Mantri as governing Hadināḍ under the orders of Kumāra Kampaṇa. He is said to be the son of Saṅgama Raja[4]. This Saṅgama cannot but be Saṅgama II. The fact that he was ruling under the orders of Kumāra Kampaṇa, the son of Bukka I, shows that the descendants of Kampa acknowledged the sovereignity of Bukka.

Not much is heard of the third brother Bukka during the lifetime of Harihara I. One of his inscriptions of the year 1378 tells us that Harihara I "appointed his younger brother Bukka-Rāja as Yuva-Rāja"[5]. On what occasion this appointment was made will be discussed later on; the fact is

Weber, *Berlin Catalogue*, I, p. 222, No. 789.

Ep. Ind., III, p. 34.

Butterworth, II, p. 847.

Ep. Carn., IV, Ch, 64. Sayana afterwards became the minister of Bukka I and Harihara II. Cf. Narasimhachar, *Madhavacharya and his Younger Brothers*, *Ind. Ant.*, XLV, p. 22.

Ep. Carn., V, Cn, 256.

that in the year 1346 a grant is recorded in the Bangalore Taluka "while the mahāmandalēśvaras, champions over kings who break their word śrī-vīra Ariyappa-Uḍaiyar (Harihara I) and Bukkaṇa-Uḍaiyar were ruling the earth"[1]. This seems to suppose that by this time Bukka had already been appointed Yuva-Rāja. We do not know how long this joint rule lasted. Sewell in 1900 supposed that Harihara I died in 1343[2]; but many new inscriptions have since been discovered, and among them there is one of the year 1355[3]. At the same time Bukka is said to be ruling from the jewelled throne at Vijayanagara[4], without any mention of his brother Harihara; and in the following year 1356 Bukka I is mentioned "with his kingdom growing by the benedictions of the good"[5]. It is therefore evident that Harihara lived till the year 1355 and that the joint rule of Harihara and Bukka lasted till this date, Bukka nevertheless being only the Yuva Rāja or heir apparent. During this period of joint rule we find the Yuva Rāja Bukka ruling at Dōrasamudra in the year 1352[6]. Was he placed there by Ballāḷa III at the time of his shifting to Tiruvaṇṇāmalai, or was he sent to the ancient Hoysaḷa capital after the death of Ballāḷa IV? We are unable to reply to these questions at the present state of research.

The fourth son of Saṅgama was Mārapa. An inscription of the year 1347 in the Sorab Taluka informs us that he

---

1 *Ep. Carn.*, IX, Bn, p. 59.

2 Sewell, *A Forgotten Empire*, p. 26.

3 *M. A. R.*, 1919, p. 23.

4 Rice, *Mysore Inscription*, p. 2 and 4; *Ep. Carn.*, XI, Cd, 2 and 3; XII, p. 74; Fleet, *P. S. & O. C. I.*, p. 21, Nos. 149 and 150; *J. B. B. R. A. S.*, XII, p. 339.

5 *Ep. Carn.*, X, Kl, 222.

6 *Madras Epigraphical Record*, 1906, p. 522.

had "acquired a kingdom in the West". His capital was Gōmanta-śaila "the excellent Chandragupti (Chandragutti)"[1]. This kingdom was the ancient Male-rājya, or hill kingdom, also called the Āraga kingdom; but Mārapa's jurisdiction also extended to the province of Haive (North Kanara), for the same inscription tells us that Chandragutti was the chief capital of "the Vanavāse (Banavāsi) Twelve Thousand kingdom"[2]. This was another strategic point in the defence of the Hoysaḷa Empire, and was most likely entrusted to Mārapa by the same Hoysaḷa king Ballaḷā III. Thus the whole northern frontier of the Hoysaḷa Empire was confided to the valour and loyalty of the sons of Saṅgama: Kampa in the east, Harihara and Bukka in the centre, and Mārapa in the west, while Bukka himself was perhaps appointed governor of the very ancient capital of the Empire, Dōrasamudra. Evidently they are some of those "his kinsmen" whom Ballāḷa had convened to prepare the defence of his Empire.

The above inscription relates that Mārapa "in order to inquire into the welfare of the people, set out on an expedition. As he was proceeding, on a certain occasion he encountered the Kādamba king, surrounded like Śakra by an army composed of elephants, horsemen and foot-soldiers". Mārapa "defeated him in battle"[3]. This Kādamba king undoubtedly was a descendant of the Kadamba Dynasty who had ruled in Banavāsi several centuries before, and who had finally been dispossessed of Banavāsi by the Hoysaḷa Emperor Vishnuvardhana. We are besides informed by the same inscription that the 'great minister' of Mārapa was Mādhava, "whose guru was Kriyāśakti, and of such fame that he was

[1] *Ep. Carn.*, VIII, Sb, 375.
[2] Ibid.
[3] Ibid.

himself Tryāmbaka"[1]. There is no doubt that this Mādhava is the great scholar Vidyāraṇya, so famous in later times as the guru of the Śringēri math. He is called "the learned Mādhava," one " who by the power of his wisdom could overreach even Guru (or Brihaspati)". It is stated furthermore that both Mārapa and Mādhava " having examined together the three Vēdas and the text of the Purānas, for love to the world and affection to the minister, he (Mārapa) gave to mankind the commandments of Tryāmbaka in the compilation *Śaivāgama-sāra*"[2]. All these praises clearly point to the great guru whose half brother was also the minister of Mārapa's brother, Kampaṇa. How long Mārapa's rule lasted in Gutti we cannot positively state. It is nevertheless a fact that the ruler of the kingdom of Gutti in the year 1367 was already Vīra Virupa (Virupaṇṇa) Rāya, son of Bukka I[3].

Nothing is heard of the fifth son of Saṅgama, Muddapa. The fact that the above mentioned Sorab inscription does not mention him at all, seems to suggest that he had already passed away in 1347, when the inscription was engraved. Nevertheless he was still alive in 1346 when all the five brothers visited the Śringeri math[4].

What were the relations among the five brothers? The above mentioned visit to the Śringeri math in 1346 proves that they were on friendly terms. Yet the main question is whether the four younger brothers acknowledged Harihara as the sovereign of all; or whether the territories individually governed by them were considered in those early

---

1 Ibid.
2 Ibid.
3 *Ep. Carn.*, VIII, Nr, 34.
4 *Ep. Carn.*, VI, Sg, 1.

days to form part of a kingdom, the capital of which was Vijayanagara. Perhaps the Bitragunta inscription may be alleged as showing this subordination of Kampa to his brother Harihara [1]. In any case the authority of Ibn Batuta seems to suppose this fact. He says that the chief of Honavar paid homage to Harihara [2]. Now Honavar was evidently included in the Chandragutti kingdom that embraced the Haive country [3]. Hence the kingdom of Chandragutti acknowledged the sovereignty of Harihara and consequently formed part of his kingdom. There is besides an inscription of the year 1347 which states that the city of Hastini (Vijayanagara) "was protected by the King Harihara together with his brothers" [4]. This phrase suggests a rudimentary Empire existing as early as 1347, whose supreme head was Harihara I, his brothers being the supporters of the same. Consequently Harihara I was recognized by his brothers as their suzerain.

8. THE HOYSALA COUNTRY AND THE FIRST VIJAYANAGARA RULERS

After considering the position occupied by the sons of Saṅgama in the last days of the Hoysaḷa Empire, the study of the relations between the first Vijayanagara rulers, Harihara and Bukka, and the Hoysaḷa country proper will disclose once more their connection with the Hoysaḷa family.

It is interesting indeed to note that during the reigns of the first two rulers of Vijayanagara we hear of no wars in the Hoysaḷa country proper, and both Harihara and Bukka

[1] *Ep. Ind.*, III, p. 32, V. 6.

[2] Defremery-Sanguinetti, *Voyages d'Ibn Batoutah*, IV, p. 68.

[3] Cf. above and *Ep. Carn.*, VIII, Sb, 375.

[4] Ibid.

are universally acknowledged in the whole present territory of Mysore. And this is specially to be emphasized, because during these two reigns several wars broke out round the old Hoysaḷa territory. We hear of wars against the Muhammadans of Madura[1], against the Muhammadans of Delhi[2], against the Telugu country[3], against Śaṅka or Śaṅkapārya in the Konkan[4] and against some petty chiefs in Haive and Barakūra-Rājya[5]; but Harihara and Bukka seem not to have been in need of waging any war in the present state of Mysore which was the centre of the Hoysaḷa country[6]. The following facts chronologically ordered will moreover disclose that both the rulers were received in the Hoysaḷa country as their natural and indisputable lords. These facts are the following:—

1346. This seems to be the date of Ballāḷa IV's death, as his last inscription is dated this year[7]. This inscription is found in the Begūr hobli, Bangalore Taluka; hence it proves that in this year the authority of Ballāḷa IV was

[1] S. Krishnaswami Aiyangar, *Sources of Vijayanagar History*, p. 23-24.

[2] *Ep. Ind.*, III, p. 32.

[3] These wars against the Telugu country will be the subject of our study in one of our later chapters.

[4] *Ep. Carn.*, V, Hn, 7; VIII, Tl, 201; XII, Tp, 9.

[5] For instance the war against the Kadamba chief spoken of above.

[6] The first war in the Hoysala country we come across in the Mysore inscriptions is during the reign of Harihara II. In 1384 he is said to have "conquered Karnata, Kuntala, Konkana, Hoysala, Andhra, Chola and Pandya kings". *M. A. R.*, 1916, p. 58. This enumeration nevertheless does not seem very reliable; it sounds like an empty boast similar to that list of ancient kings Bhojas, Cambhojas, Kalingas and Karahatas defeated by other sovereigns.

[7] *Ep. Carn.*, IX, Bn, 120.

acknowledged in the surroundings of Bangalore. Now in the same year, most likely after the death of Ballāḷa IV, the authority of Harihara was recognized in the same Taluka, according to an inscription at the Vartūr hobli[1]. Three years before another inscription at the same hobli refers to Ballāḷa III as the lawful sovereign of the place[2]. Thus after the disappearance of the last representative of the Hoysaḷa family, the authority of Harihara I is at once acknowledged in the south-east of Mysore.

In the same year a Tamil inscription at the Malūr Taluka, Kolar District, records a remission of taxes by order of Harihara, who receives the following birūdas: "The subduer of hostile kings, champion over kings who break their word". The order moreover is said to be issued "with the royal seal"[3]. All this confirms the fact that Harihara I was recognized in the east of Mysore in the very year of the death of Ballāḷa IV.

But the most interesting event in this respect is the visit of Harihara with his brothers and some relations paid to the Śringeri math in the Kadūr District, west of Mysore. "The mahāmaṇḍalēśvara, subduer of hostile kings, champion over kings who break their word, vīra-Hariyapoḍeyar, Kampaṇṇoḍeyar, Mārapoḍeyar, Muddapoḍeyar, son-in-law Ballappadaṇṇāyaka, Kumāra Sōvannoḍeyar and others made to Bhāratī-tīrtha-śrīpāda, his disciples and others, and the forty Brāhmaṇs residing in that tīrtha of Śringeri, for the performance of rites and service, a grant on a stone śāsana". The inscription moreover states that "Harihara having conquered the earth from the eastern to the western ocean, in order to

[1] *Ep. Carn.*, IX, Bn, 47.
[2] Ibid., 40.
[3] *Ep. Carn.*, X, Mr, 39.

celebrate the festival of his victory", made this grant [1]. This visit is also spoken of in another inscription of 1380, in the reign of Harihara II: "When Hiriya Hariyapp-Oḍeyar was ruling the earth in the Hoysaṇa country, he came along with his brothers and son-in-law Billappa-daṇṇāyaka to Śrīngēri to pay homage to Vidyātīrtha-śrīpāda in the year Pārthiva (1346)" [2]. From the study of these two passages we may draw the following conclusions:—

1. Harihara I with his brothers, his son-in-law (the nephew and minister of Ballāḷa III) and a prince and some other people (perhaps relatives) went to the Śringeri math in the year 1346, apparently after the death of Ballāḷa IV.

2. In the Śringeri śāsana recording this event Harihara is given the same birūdas as in the east of Mysore; hence he is acknowledged as the ruler of the country from the east to the west of Mysore.

3. The visit was paid by Harihara and his brothers and relations and the grant was made in order to celebrate a great event. This event is called 'victory,' and it is evident from the context that such victory was nothing else than the conquest of "the earth from the eastern to the western ocean".

4. This conquest is called conquest and victory in a very broad sense. A real victory and conquest supposes an enemy, and this enemy is always mentioned in the inscriptions of those days: the Turushkas, the Chōḷas, the Paṇḍyas, the Telingas, the lord of Kuntala, Śanka of Konkan, etc. Now since the enemy is not mentioned on this occasion, it is evident that the enemy did not exist, a fact which is confirmed by the absence of records testifying the conquest of the

[1] *Ep. Carn.*, VI, Sg, 1.
[2] *M. A. R.*, 1916, p. 56-57.

southern portion of the peninsula from the eastern to the western ocean. This phrase is therefore a stereotyped expression meaning that Harihara obtained the sovereignty over "the earth from the eastern to the western ocean".

5. This sovereignty over the Hoysaḷa country acquired without any battle in the same year of the death of Ballāḷa IV clearly shows that Harihara became the heir to the Hoysaḷa throne, possibly because of the exalted post which he was in charge of on the northern frontier; most likely because of the close relationship existing between Ballāḷa and Harihara.

1352. In this year we find Bukka I ruling at Dōrasamudra, the old capital of the Hoysaḷa Empire[1].

1354-5. The same Bukka I makes a grant of a village close to Harihar to an astrologer. In it he receives the following birūdas: "The glorious king Bukka, the fortunate king of Victory, the supreme king of great kings"[2].

1355. An inscription at the Hoskote Taluka, Bangalore District, mentions one Vajiyanna "who was the house merchant of the mahāmaṇḍalēśvara Harihara Rāya Oḍeyar"[3]. Another inscription at the Chitaldrug District also recognizes the authority of "the mahāmaṇḍalēśvara Śrī Bukkarāya Voḍeya... ruling at his capital Hosapaṭṭana in the Hoysaṇa country"[4]. The birūdas that Bukka receives in this inscription are the following: "A destroyer of rulers, the conqueror of opposing kings, the punisher of kings who break their word, the lord of the eastern and western oceans". The same inscription extols Bukka as the greatest king of the Karnaṭaka country in the following way: "Beyond the reach

[1] *Madras Epigraphical Record*, 1906, p. 522.
[2] *J. B. B. R. A. S.*, XII, p. 338, 350.
[3] *M. A. R.*, 1919, p. 33.
[4] *J. B. B. R. A. S.*, XII, p. 339; *P. S. & O. C. I.*, p. 21, No. 149.

of slander, a thunderbolt to the mountain chains the hostile kings, is Bukka Rāya, at the brandishing of whose glittering sword the earth trembles, kings steal away in terror and hide themselves; by their evil designs they bring ruin on themselves and are beaten however strong. What king in truth can stand before him ? A lion to the rutting elephants the hostile kings, a crowning ornament of the wisest monarchs, firm as mount Mēru, delighting in battle with opposing kings, the treasury to which all kings and rulers come, who, O Bukka Rāya, among the kings of the earth is king above you?"[1]. All this seems to suppose that Bukka was the only king at Vijayanagara, at least towards the end of 1355. In fact Harihara seems to have died in the course of this year as he is not mentioned any more in the inscriptions.

1356. Bukka I again visits the Śringeri math and makes a grant of lands situated in Satāḷige-naḍu, and Kinkunda-naḍu and Kella-naḍu, all apparently in the Kadūr District[2]. Another inscription in the Chitaldroog District reveals that he is still acknowledged there[3].

1365. Kumāra Kampaṇa, the son of Bukka, is acknowledged in the South Arcot District, Jinji Taluka[4].

1368. Bukka I settles a dispute between Jainas and Vaishnavas in the surroundings of Mysore and the terms of the settlement are engraved at Śravana Belgola[5]. In another inscription in the same District he is said to be on "the south side of the Kavēri, in the country of the strong armed king Vishnuvardhana pratāpa Hoysaḷa"[6].

---

[1] Rice, *Mysore Inscriptions*, p. 2 and 3.

[2] *M. A. R.*, 1916, p. 56 and 57.

[3] *J. B. B. R. A. S.*, XII, p. 340; Fleet, *P. S. & O. C. I.*, p. 150.

[4] 52 of 1905.

[5] *Ep. Carn.*, II, 344; IX, Ma, 18.

[6] *Ep. Carn.*, IV, Ch, 113.

1369. Kampaṇa, Bukka's son, is also recognized as lawful ruler of the Tirukkōyilur Taluka, South Arcot District[1].

1371. Bukka I is called "the destroyer of hostile kings, master of the four oceans", in an inscription of the Shimoga District[2], and consequently still acknowledged in that District. Another inscription testifies that the chief Bodha-mahādeva, in Hassan, acknowledged Bukka as his paramount lord. Bodha-mahādeva is said to be the chief of Durga[3].

1373. Kumāra Kampaṇa is still acknowledged in the Tirukkōyilur Taluka[4], and also in the Vriddhachalam Taluka of the same District[5].

1375. Bukka is again mentioned as continuing his rule over the Bangalore District[6].

1376. Bukka is called "Suratrana of Hindu Rajas", by an inscription in the Bangalore Taluka, a phrase that seems to indicate that he was even acknowledged by some petty chiefs[7]. In the Sorab Taluka there is another inscription recording a sati "in the reign of vīra-Bukka-Rāya"[8].

These facts evidently prove that the first Vijayanagara rulers, without waging any war, had become the natural lords of the Hoysaḷa dominions. Some other inscriptions of later days show again the same. Two cases will suffice to illustrate our statement:—

---

1 165 of 1904.
2 *Ep. Carn.*, VIII, Sb, 17.
3 *Ep. Carn.*, VI, Mg, 87. Cf. *Ep. Carn.*, I, Cg, p. 19.
4 29 of 1905.
5 13 of 1903.
6 *Ep. Carn.*, IX, Dv, 13.
7 *Ep. Carn.*, IX, Bn, 132.
8 *Ep. Carn.*, VIII, Sb, 106.

(a) In 1316, during the reign of Ballāḷa III one Māra-Dēva was ruling Vanuigahalli in the Sigala-nāḍ, according to an inscription of the Kankanhalli Taluka, Bangalore District[1]. In 1391, while Harihara II was reigning, Siddaya, son of the Sigala-nāḍ mahāprābhu, son of Aralahāḷ Mārapa is said to be the minister of...Voḍeyar, son of Bukka Rāya I[2]. And two years later, in 1393, Chikka-Ariyaṇṇa, another son of the Sigala-nāḍ mahāprābhu Arulahāḷ Māragauḍa acknowledges the mahāmaṇḍalēśvara Narana Dēva Voḍeyar, a Viceroy of Vijayanagara[3].

(b) In 1553 Lingaṇṇa Nāyaka, who recognizes Sadāśiva Rāya in an inscription of the Kadūr District, says that the Dānivāsa-śime was granted to his family by vīra Hoysaḷa Ballāḷa mahārāya[4].

9. LOYALTY OF THE VIJAYANAGARA RULERS TO THE HOYSALA EMPERORS.

After the tragic end of Ballāḷa III in 1342 his son Ballāḷa IV ascended the throne[5]. He seems to have died in 1346, as this is the last date of his inscriptions[6], and apparently he was the last member of the main line of his family. We spoke above of another so-called son of Ballāḷa III, named Vīra Sōmapa-Daṇṇāyaka[7]; but he seems to be rather a nephew than a son of the Hoysaḷa Emperor. An inscription of 1340 mentions another son of Ballāḷa III, named Mayili

[1] *Ep. Carn.*, IX, Kn, 104.
[2] *Ep. Carn.*, IX, Kn, 98.
[3] Ibid., 100.
[4] *Ep. Carn.*, VI, Kp, 17.
[5] *Ep. Carn.*, VI, Cm, 105.
[6] *Ep. Carn.*, IX, Bn, 120.
[7] *Ep. Carn.*, IX, Kl, 104.

Nāyaka. He is called "mahā-sāvantā-Dhipati, champion over the world of man"[1]. It is difficult to say whether he was the real son of the Hoysaḷa Emperor, or only his nephew. In any case even supposing that he was Ballāḷa's son, the fact that no other mention of his name is found in later inscriptions seems to suggest that his life was not long and he died before Ballāḷa IV. Another son of Ballāḷa III is called Hampe Voḍeyar in an inscription of 1342[2]. Mr. H. Krishna Sastri identifies him with the same Ballāḷa IV[3]; and though he gives no reasons for such an identification, his opinion is not totally unfounded. Indeed in the abishēka inscription of Ballāḷa IV, this king is called Vīra Virūpāksha Ballāḷa Dēva[4]; this seems to be the royal name taken perhaps after his abishēka. Now, Vīra Virūpāksha is the name with which the newly enlarged and fortified city of Hampe-Hastināvati was christened by Ballāḷa III. Considering moreover that Voḍeyar is the surname given on many occasions to the princes of the blood royal, one is thoroughly justified in stating that Hampe Voḍeyar is the name of the Prince son of Ballāḷa III, who after his abishēka receives the name of Vīra Virūpāksha Ballāḷa Dēva. Besides no other mention of Hampe Voḍeyar is to be found in the inscriptions. Mr. Krishna Sastri's identification, therefore, is well founded.

The fact is that the year 1346 witnessed the end of the Hoysaḷa dynasty; and it was perhaps on this occasion that Harihara I appointed Bukka his Yuva Rāja. We say perhaps, for the inscription referring to this event is of the year 1378, when Bukka himself was already on the throne after his brother Harihara's death. It is moreover a striking fact that an

---

1 *Ep. Carn.*, IX, Ma, 81.
2 *Ep. Carn.*, IV, Yd, 29.
3 *Q. J. M. S.*, II, p. 129.
4 *Ep. Carn.*, VI, Cm, 105.

inscription of the same year of Ballāḷa IV's death was written "while the mahāmaṇḍalēśvaras, champions over kings who break their word, śrī-vīra Aryiappa-uḍaiyar and Bukkaṇa-uḍaiyar were ruling the earth" [2]. This seems to indicate that Bukka was already the Yuva Rāja in the very year of the decease of the last member of the Hoysaḷa family. Till this year 1346 both Harihara[3] and Bukka[4] are called mahāmaṇḍalēśvaras, as they were evidently subordinate to the Hoysaḷa Emperor. It is nevertheless inexplicable at first sight that this humble title is still retained in the following years, when there were no more Hoysaḷa Emperors on the throne of Karṇaṭaka: Harihara I is still called mahāmaṇḍalēśvara in a few inscriptions till the end of his life [5]; and Bukka I is also styled mahāmaṇḍalēśvara in many inscriptions [6]; sometimes he

---

1 *Ep. Carn.*, V, Cn, 256.

2 *Ep. Carn.*, IX, Bn, 59.

3 Inscriptions of two years:—
1339-40. *Ind. Ant.*, X, p. 63.
1346. *Ep. Carn.*, VI, Sg, 1; VIII, Tl, 154; IX, Bn, 47, 59; X, Mr, 61.

4 Inscriptions of two years:—
1344. *Ep. Carn.*, X, Ct, 89.
1346. *Ep. Carn.*, IX, Bn, 59.

5 Inscriptions of three years:—
1347. *Ep. Carn.*, IX, Bn, 97.
1354. *Ep. Carn.*, VIII, Sb, 104.
1355. *M. A. R.*, 1919, p. 33.

6 Inscriptions of eighteen years:—
1347. *M. A. R.*, 1914-15, p. 57.
1348. *Ep. Carn.*, IX, Dv, 50
1355. *Ep. Carn.*, XI, Cd, 2; Rice, *Mysore Inscriptions*, p. 2 and 4.
1355-6. *J. B. B. R. A. S.*, XII, p. 340.
1356-7. Ibid.
1358. *Ep. Carn.*, IX, Dv, 27.

is only called Bukka Rāya without any title[1]; other times he is named Bukkabhūpati Rayal[2]; in one he is styled 'Prince'[3], and in another he is likewise called 'the great chieftain'[4]. But he never assumes the title of mahārājadhirāja. Even Bukka's son, Harihara II, in an inscription of the year 1399-1400 gives his father the same title 'mahāmaṇḍaleśvara'[5].

The meaning of this title attributed to the first Vijayanagara rulers, specially after the death of Ballāḷa IV, has never to my mind been rightly explained. Smith, for instance, while saying that "Harihara II was tha first really independent sovereign of Vijayanagara," because he "assumed full royal state or titles"[6], evidently implies that Harihara I and

---

1360. *Ep. Carn.*, III, Md, 90; Sg, 87; X, Ct, 75.
1362. *Ep. Carn.*, IX, An, 82.
1363. *Ep. Carn.*, IV, Ch, 117.
1365. *Ep. Carn.*, IX, Bn, 67.
1366. *Ep. Carn.*, X, Kl, 162; *M. A. R.*, 1917, p. 47.
1367. *Ep. Carn.*, III, Nj, 117; VIII, Nr, 34; IX, Hk, 117; DB, 39; X,Mr, 79.
1368. *Ep. Carn.*, IV, Ch, 113; Gu, 46; IX, Bn, 27; Ma, 18.
1369. *Ep. Carn.*, IV, Yl, 64; VI, Kp, 6.
1371. *Ep. Carn.*, X, CB, 63.
1374. *Ep. Carn.*, IX, Hk, 157; Nl, 53.
1376. *Ep. Carn.*, IX, An, 29; Bn, 132.
1379. *Ep. Carn.*, Hk, 108, 109.

1 Inscriptions of two years:—
1359. *Ep. Carn.*, IX, NL, 23.
1371. *Ep. Carn.*, VI, Mg, 87.

2 Inscriptions of two years:—
1366. *Ep. Carn.*, XII, Pg, 18.
1394. Ibid., 72.

3 1357. *Ep. Carn.*, V, Ag, 68.

4 1356. *P. S. & O. C. I.*, No. 15.

5 *J. B. B. R. A. S.*, XII, p. 340.

6 Smith, *Oxford History of India*, p. 302. (2nd edition).

Bukka I, who were only called mahāmaṇḍalēśvaras, were not independent. And indeed after the death of Ballāḷa IV, there is no king in the Karnaṭaka country on whom they could depend [1]. The title, therefore, was only used out of respect and loyalty to the memory of the Hoysaḷa Emperors whose subjects they had been. Even some of the successors of Bukka I used at times the same title; Harihara II appears with the title of mahāmaṇḍalēśvara six times [2], and Dēva Rāya II once; in the same inscription he is called mahāmaṇḍalēśvara and mahārājadhirāja [3]. It was something like the title of Nizam, granted originally to the founder of the Hydarabad Dynasty by the Mughal Emperor, and which is kept down to the present days out of respect for the Mughal Empire and for those past days. The title of mahāmaṇḍalēśvara among the Vijayanagara Emperors did not last so long. The above data show that after the death of Bukka I it was rapidly dying out; and we have not come across any other instance of it after the reign of Dēva Rāya II.

It has been said above that Harihara I and his brother

As a matter of fact if we are to believe the inscriptions, Harihara had several feudatory chiefs who acknowledged him as their suzerain "The rulers of mankind", we read in one of them, "did service to him ever fulfilling his commands (which they bore) as if they were garlands on their heads" *J. B. B. R. A. S.*, XII, p. 373. One of these rulers was the chief of Honavar. As regards Bukka I, an inscription of 1359 calls him "Suratana of the Hindu Rayas". *Ep. Carn.*, V, Bl, 25.

Inscriptions of five years:—

1378. *Ep. Carn.*, VIII, Sb, 200; X, Sd, 112.
1381. *Ep. Carn.*, IX, Bn, 73.
1386. Ibid., 139.
1388. *Ep. Carn.*, X, Bp, 17.
1410. *Ep. Carn.*, VI, Mg, 85.

Ep. Carn., X, Gd, 17.

Bukka never assumed imperial titles, and it is true. Nevertheless the title of mahārājadhirāja is once attributed to Harihara in 1343[1] and once to Bukka in 1368[2]. This may be a mistake of the engraver, or would in the second case prove that Bukka I was an independent sovereign; yet the title was not officially adopted by those kings, and both inscriptions are mere exceptions.

This loyalty and faithfulness of the Emperors of Vijayanagara to the memory of Hoysaḷa Emperors is also to be seen in many other inscriptions. The Vijayanagara rulers, even down to the end of the fourth Dynasty, seem to take special care never to forget that they were the political descendants of the Hoysaḷas; and thus Harihara I[3], Bukka I[4] Harihara II[5], Bukka II[6], Mallikārjuna[7], Virūpāksha[8], Kṛishṇa, Dēva Rāya[9], Achyuta Dēva Rāya[10], Rāma II[11], and Veṅkaṭa IV down to 1669[12] often state in their inscriptions that they rule the earth in the Hoysaḷa country or kingdom. The Hoy-

[1] *Ep. Carn.*, V, Ak, 159. This title may be easily explained: at the time of the death of Ballala III it was perhaps supposed that Harihara would take imperial titles.

[2] *Ep. Carn.*, VII, Sk, 281.

[3] *M. A. R.*, 1916, p. 56-57.

[4] *Ep. Carn.*, VIII, Nr, 34; IX, Nl, 53; Rice, *Mysore Inscriptions*, p. 2 and 4; *J. B. B. R. A. S.*, XII, p. 340; *P. S. & O. C. I.*, p. 21, No. 149.

[5] *Ep. Carn.*, IV, Ch, 114; V, Bl, 148; Hn, 36; *M. A. R.*, 1912-13, p. 43

[6] *Ep. Carn.*, IV, Hg, 1; V, Cn, 256.

[7] *Ep. Carn.*, V, Sg, 11.

[8] *Ep. Carn.*, V, Ag, 41.

[9] *Ep. Carn.*, V, Bl, 79.

[10] *Ep. Carn.*, XI, Hk, 132.

[11] *Ep. Carn.*, XII, Ck, 1.

[12] *Ep. Carn.*, XII, Ck, 38.

saḷa army is also mentioned in three inscriptions of Bukka I[1]; and in another inscription of this king he is said to be ruling "in the country of the strong-armed king Vishnuvardhana pratāpa-Hoysaḷa"[2]. Some of the birūdas given to the Vijayanagara Emperors greatly resemble the Hoysaḷa birūdas, and seem in fact to be copied from their inscriptions, Bukka I is called "the pearl of the heroes of the race of Yādu" [3]. Harihara II is styled "boon lord of Dvārāvatī-pura" [4]. And Dēva Rāya II is said to be "the maintainer of the orders of the old kings of the Hoysaḷa-nāḍ"[5].

But the loyalty of the Vijayanagara Emperors towards the Hoysaḷa sovereigns is more evident in their doings than in these phrases and feelings. The political inheritance they received from the Hoysaḷas pointed to the Muhammadans both of the north and of the south. The Sultans of Delhi had been the implacable enemies of the Hoysaḷa Empire, and the Sultan of Madura had defeated the great Vīra Ballāḷa III and caused him to be mercilessly slain. Both enemies were to be met with not long after the extinction of the Hoysaḷa familyt. The Bitragunta inscriptions of Saṅgama II, of the year 1356, says: "By whom (Harihara I) the Suratrāṇa (Sultan), who resembled Sutrāman (Indra), was conquered"[6]. It is therefore evident that already in the year 1356 Harihara had inflicted a defeat upon the Sultan. Who was this Sultan it is not clear. Yet since the expedition of Kumāra Kampaṇa against the Sultan of Madura is the first war of Vijayanagara

1 *Ep. Carn.*, XI, Cd, 2; Rice, *Mysore Inscriptions*, p. 2 and 4.
2 *Ep. Carn.*, IV, Ch, 113.
3 *J. B. B. R. A. S.*, XII, p. 373.
4 *Ep. Carn.*, VII, Ci, 28.
5 *Ep. Carn.*, III, TN, 55.
6 *Ep. Ind.*, III, p. 32.

against the Southern Mussulmans, it is evident that the Sultan defeated by Harihara is a Northern Sultan. It could be Muhammad bin Tuglak, or perhaps Alla-ud-din Hassan Shah Gangu Bahmani, the first Sultan of Galbarga, who had rebelled against the power of Delhi in 1347. In any case the Mussulman power of the north was successfully checked by Harihara, according to the wishes of Ballāḷa III. As regards the south, the above mentioned expedition of Kumāra Kampaṇa, a son of Bukka I, was so successful that no remnant of Mussulman power in Madura was to be found at the time of Bukka I's death[1]. The cruel death of Ballaḷa III was thus revenged.

Moreover the great devotion of Harihara II to the god Kēśava of Belur, the chief shrine of the Hoysaḷa Empire, founded by the great monarch Vishnuvardhana is a striking and noteworthy fact. A stone śāsana at Belur of the year 1380—the first year of Harihara II's reign—according to which king Harihara made gifts to the Brahmans of this city, contains the following praises of, and prayers to, the above god. "The god Kēśava grant us happiness, who, in the time of the illustrious Hoisaṇa kings, adorned with the collection of all good qualities, conspicuous for bodily strength—as if the divine Vishnu sought how to obtain similar fortune—took upon himself the plan of the protection of all the world in Velanagara, the city of his servant. The god Kēśava of Velapura, giver of sight to the blind, who raises up the poor to royal dignity, who causes the lame to be the swiftest of the swift, makes the dumb as eloquent as Brihaspati, the barren to be crowded with offspring, the granter of all desires, alike to the residents of that country and the foreign-

---

[1] Cf. Heras, *The Aravidu Dynasty of Vijayanagara*, I, p. 103-4.

ers from abroad, protect us. The great god Kēśava protect us, the god whom the wise Nārada hymned as follows: 'O destroyer of sin, god of gods, the supreme, remover of all sorrow, the merciful'; who dwells, the first original body of the god, in the city of Velapura, which is a shore to check the rising waters of pride"[1].

One year after, in 1381, the great minister Kampaṇṇa restored a portion of the same temple of Kēśava at Belur, and set up four pillars with capitals "by order of the rājādhirāja paramēśvara vīra-Harihara-Rāya"[2]. In 1397 Harihara again repairs another portion of the temple, and by his order, Gunda Daṇḍanātha "restored the grants which Vishnuvardhana-Biṭṭi-Dēva-Rāya, ruler of the Hoysaṇa country, had made for the god Chenna-Kēśavanātha, his family god, and which had by lapse of time been greatly reduced"[3].

There is finally one inscription that proves the great respect of the Vijayanagara rulers for the memory of their Hoysaḷa predecessors, and perhaps even confirms the opinion that both the families come from the same stock, whose head was Saḷa. During the reign of Bukka I, apparently in 1359, or shortly before, somebody (who he was it is not clear, for the inscription is much defaced) demanded from the king the town of Sosavūru "situated in the Kali-nadiyama-nāḍ Four-thousand, which is reckoned the Kākare-nāḍ of the Pariya-ghaṭṭa (Western Ghats)". Sosavūru was the town where the origin of the Hoysaḷa family took place. Accordingly two ministers of Bukka, Teppada-Nāgaṇṇa-Voḍeyar and Tipaṇṇa-Voḍeyar, undoubtedly acting on behalf of their

1 Rice, *Mysore Inscriptions*, p. 226.
2 *Ep. Carn.*, V, Bl, 52.
3 Ibid., 3.

monarch were "unwilling to give up Sosavūru"[1]. And the birth place of the Hoysaḷa family remained in the possession of the Emperors of Vijayanagara till the end of the Empire.

All these facts prove beyond doubt that the Vijayanagara Emperors considered themselves as political heirs of the Hoysaḷas; accordingly their interior and exterior policy was but an extension of the policy of Vishnuvardhana and Ballāḷa III.

10. THE FIRST VIJAYANAGARA EMPERORS AND THE TELUGU COUNTRY.

This is another side-issue to be studied in the early history of Vijayanagara; for after considering the relations between the first rulers of Vijayanagara and the Hoysaḷa country, the study of the relations between the same sovereigns and the Telugu country will disclose what was their affection for this country and its people, from where they were once supposed to come.

Besides the Bitragunta grant of Saṅgama II not much information is available about the Telugu country during the reign or Harihara I. An inscription of his reign states that he "conquered the whole world, beginning with the Aṅgas and Kalingas"[2]. This war seems to have been very successful, for another inscription of the same monarch informs us that he "was served by the kings of Aṅga, Kalinga and other countries"[3]. Yet after the death of Harihara, the Andhra country apparently rebelled against Bukka I. For most of the inscriptions of Bukka I refer to a war against the Telugu

---

[1] *Ep. Carn.*, VI, Mg, 25. The Hoysalas themselves had this place in great veneration. Cf. Rice, *Mysore and Coorg*, p. 99.

[2] Butterworth, o. c., I, p. 113.

[3] *Ep. Carn.*, X, Bg, 70.

country. This evidently shows that a rebellion against Bukka occurred in the Telugu country, which was crushed by the monarch. More than any comment, the words of the inscriptions themselves will perhaps disclose the importance of this event, as regards the origin of Bukka's family. The different samples of wording are quoted below:—

1. In the reign of Bukka I "the Andhras ran into caves ... the Kalingas suffered defeat" [1].

2. During Bukka's resign "the Kalingas were broken through his valour ... the Andhras ran into holes" [2].

3. "As Bukka danced round the field of battle ... the Andhras ran into holes ... the Kalingas suffered defeat" [3].

4. "As he (Bukka I) danced about on the battle field... the Andhras ran into holes. . .the Kalingas were broken" [4].

5. "As he (Bukka I) danced about on the battle field, the Andhras went into holes in the frontier hills. . .the Kalingas were broken" [5].

6. When his (Bukka I's) sword began to dance on the battle field. . .the Andhras ran into caves. . .the Kalingas suffered defeat" [6].

7 "As his (Bukka I's) sword danced about on the battle field, ... the Andhras ran into caves in the direction of Udayagiri, ... the Kalingas were defeated" [7].

8. "As the point of his (Bukka I's) sword danced

Ep. Carn., V, Hn, 70.
Ep. Carn., X, Gd, 46.
Ep. Carn., III, TN, 134.
Ep. Carn., XII, Tp, 9.
Ep. Carn., VIII, Tl, 201.
Ep. Carn., V, HN, 7.
Ep. Carn., VII, Ci, 13.

about. . .the Andhras sought the shelter of caves . . . the Kalingas suffered defeat" [1].

9. "When he (Bukka I) flourished his sword on the battle field . . . the Andhras . . . and the Kalingas fled in terror"[2].

10. While Bukka I was on the throne "broken were the Kalingas, with small display of courage . . . the Andhras hid themselves in holes from the blows of the cruel weapons of his arms" [3].

All these phrases evidently refer to the same event, *viz.* a defeat of the Telugu people, by the army of Bukka I. Accordingly another inscription informs us that Bukka I "having conquered in all points of the compass, he was served by the kings of Aṅga (and) Kalinga" [4]. This subjection nevertheless apparently did not last long. Perhaps after the death of Bukka the Telugus again rebelled against Vijayanagara, for Harihara II is also said to have defeated them as early as 1397. The expressions found in the inscriptions as regards this third defeat are the following:—

1. "Into the flames of his (Harihara II's) valour the Yavana, Turushka and Āndhra hostile kings fell like moths" [5].

2. "Having conquered the Kēralas, Tauluvas, Andhras and Kutakas, he (Guṇda Daṇḍanātha) seized their wealth and gave it to his king (Harihara II)" [6].

[1] *Ep. Carn.*, VI, Kp, 25.
[2] *M. A. R.*, 1916, p. 59.
[3] *Ep. Carn.*, X, Mb, 158.
[4] *Ep. Carn.*, X, Bg, 70.
[5] *Ep. Carn.*, V, Bl, 3.
[6] Ibid.

3. "Andhra went blind ... Kalinga bolted from the field, Andhra took refuge in a mountain cave"[1].

4. "Upon whom (Harihara II) the ... Kalinga ... kings waited as servants, holding the chāmaras and other royal insignia"[2].

This third defeat of the Telugus in the reign of Harihara II, inflicted this time by Harihara's minister Guṇḍa Daṇḍanātha, took place in the last year of the XIVth century. Accordingly in the year 1401 a pilgrimage of Telugus to the court of Vijayanagara is mentioned in an inscription at the Tumkur District[3]. Another inscription in the same District of the year 1419 refers to another Telugu pilgrimage to the city of Vijayanagara[4]. Evidently such pilgrimages did not take place before peace was settled between Vijayanagara and the Telugu country.

These rebellions of the Telugu country against the early Vijayanagara rulers prove that the latter were not acknowledged by the Telugus, a thing which can hardly be believed if the family of Saṅgama is supposed to be a Telugu family. In any case it is worth noticing the different attitude offered by the Telugu and the Kanarese country towards the early Vijayanagara sovereigns. The Kanarese country, once the Hoysaḷas have totally disappeared, acknowledge the sons of Saṅgama as the only legitimate masters of the country; while the Telugu country thrice rebelled against them, and did not recognize them except forcibly and unwillingly.

These Telugu wars offer moreover on the part of the Vijayanagara rulers themselves another point of contact be-

---

[1] Ibid.

[2] *Ep. Carn.*, IX, Hk, 34.

[3] *Ep. Carn.*, XII, Pg, 82.

[4] *Ep. Carn.*, XII, Pg, 96.

tween them and the Hoysaḷa Emperors. For several of the Emperors of that dynasty had also fought against the Telugus, as is to be seen in the expressions quoted below, which seem to have offered a model to the authors of the Vijayanagara inscriptions quoted above:—

Vishnuvardhana.

"He broke the bones of the . . . Kalinga"[1].

"Andhra hid in a hole for an ambush"[2].

Narasiṁha.

"Kalinga went to dwell in the forest"[3].

"When he mounted his horse for an expedition of victory, Kalinga went away to live in the woods"[4].

Ballaḷā II.

"Kalinga went off to live in the woods"[5].

"Khaṉiṅga (Kalinga) went to live in the forest"[6].

"Putter down of the pride of the Andhra king"[7].

"When he mounted his horse for an expedition of victory, Kalinga went off to live in the forest"[8].

Siṁhana Dēva.

"Plucker up by the roots of the lotus, the head of the Kalinga king"[9].

[1] *Ep. Carn.*, V, Cn, 179.
[2] Ibid., Ak, 62.
[3] Ibid., 157.
[4] *Ep. Carn.*, XII, Tp, 128.
[5] *Ep. Carn.*, V, Ak, 138.
[6] Ibid., 62.
[7] *Ep. Carn.*, V, Cn, 179.
[8] Ibid., 265.
[9] *Ep. Carn.*, VII, Sk, 95.

CONCLUSION

While the two preceding lectures were being printed, my attention was drawn to a few inscriptions which had first escaped my notice. Some comments upon these documents seem to be necessary here to supplement the information given in the course of the lectures.

Several times in the preceding pages, the meeting of Ballāḷa III with his kinsmen, in order to defend the Empire against the Muhammadans, has been mentioned. Ferishta, who is the only one that speaks of this assembly, does not mention at all the place and the date of it. But after the study of several contemporary inscriptions, I wrote the following lines in my second lecture:—

"The first change of capital, according to the above table, took place in 1328, when Ballāḷa transferred his residence from Dōrasamudra to Uṇṇāmalepaṭṭaṇa, *i. e.* Tiruvaṇṇāmalai. This date seems to coincide with the conquest of Warangal by the Mussulmans and the meeting of Kṛishṇa Nāyaka with Ballāḷa III referred to by Ferishta. It was therefore most likely at Tiruvaṇṇāmalai that the assembly of Ballāḷa III with his kinsmen in order to defend the Empire against the Muhammadans was held"[1].

Accordingly Tiruvaṇṇāmalai was suggested as the probable place of the assembly summoned by Ballāḷa III, and the year 1328 seemed to be the date of that event.

---

[1] Supra, pp. 66-67.

One of the inscriptions that was unfortunately overlooked during the preparation of the above lectures is one that comes from the Chitaldroog Taluka, dated in the same year 1328. The epigraph commemorates the setting up of a linga in Bemmaturakallu by the two generals Ballapa-daṇṇāyaka and Singeya-daṇṇāyaka. Furthermore the document records that this event took place "when the Hoysaṇa strong-armed vīra-Ballāḷa-Dēva, together with the champion at his side, the strong-armed Bhīma-Rāya, the prince Kaṭhōra-Hara, the prince Siṁha-Raghunātha, the prince Kāḷamēgha, the prince Vīra-Śānta, Baicheya-daṇṇāyaka-chamūpa, who was the punisher of the famous Mādhava Rāya of Udevāra, the great minister Ballapa-daṇṇāyaka and the great minister Singeya daṇṇāyaka, were in the residence of the city of Uṇṇamale ruling the kingdom in peace and wisdom" [1].

While studying this interesting passage it is to be noted first of all that the two ministers who erected the linga, and who therefore ordered the inscription to be engraved, were also two of those noblemen who were ruling the kingdom together with King Ballāḷa III. Hence we cannot say that the phrase 'ruling the kingdom' was an exaggeration of a person not well acquainted with the facts referred to. Hence the meaning of this phrase is to be investigated. Certainly it cannot mean that all those nobles and ministers together with the King were ruling the kingdom with royal authority as the King himself was ruling it. It undoubtedly means that they were ruling the kingdom as in an assembly, where their advice and their personal assistance were required by the King; and since this is the only inscription among those belonging to the Hoysaḷa Emperors, in which so many per-

---

[1] *Ep. Carn.*, XI, Cd, 4.

sons are represented as 'ruling the kingdom', one may safely state that this assembly of nobles, some of them apparently princes of the blood royal, was an assembly convoked for an emergency case to decide about matters of great importance, in connection with the safety and life of the Empire.

All this seems to point to the meeting of his kinsmen convened by Ballāḷa III, as Ferishta mentions. And it is interesting to notice that the place and the date of the meeting are respectively Uṇṇāmale, *i. e.* Tiruvaṇṇāmalai, and 1328. Such are precisely, the place and the date of Ballāḷa's meeting with his kinsmen suggested in the above lecture.

One of the kinsmen of Ballāḷa attending this meeting, according to the inscription, was prince Kaṭhōra-Hara. This name properly means 'the fierce Śiva'. Can it not be supposed that this prince, Kaṭhōra-Hara, was the future Harihara I of Vijayanagara, who in all probability was one of those kinsmen of Ballāḷa, summoned to the meeting of Tirivaṇṇāmalai? If that is so, if Kaṭhōra-Hara is Harihara, the opinion that states the relationship between Ballāḷa and Harihara will be strengthened. For Harihara is to be one of those kinsmen summoned by the old Emperor; specially as he is mentioned the first among all the princes after the champion at Ballāḷa's side, the strong-armed Bhīma-Rāya[1].

On many occasions Harihara's name is cut short and only the first part is given, thus Hariyappa. Perhaps on this occasion the first part is omitted, so that the epithet Kathora (fierce) should be properly applied to Hara or Siva. In fact Kathora is the thirty-seventh name of Siva. This would be a welcome piece of flattery for Harihara.

The second inscription that was overlooked in the course of the lectures is an inscription of the year 1309, found in the Shimoga Taluka. This document refers to the exemption of taxes in the time of Ballāḷa III. The most important person mentioned in this epigraph after the Emperor is one Dēvappa-Hariyappa. He is said to be "the *sarvvādhikāri*, (minister or governor) of Haḍavaḷike-nāḍ". This country is said to be in Gaṅga Maṇḍala and from the context of the inscription it is evident that it was in the District of Shimoga, Kusugūr being one of the important towns. On the other hand Dēvappa Hariyappa, the governor of this nāḍ, is said to be "the strong man of Lakkaṇṇa, the minister for peace and war of that king's house" [1]. All this points to a great state officer in the kingdom of Ballāḷa III, in the beginning of the XIVth century. Was this Dēvappa Hariyappa, the same Hariyappa or Harihara I who was some years later placed as his mahāmandalēśvara in the most difficult post of the northern frontier by Ballāḷa III? This important post confided to him seems to suppose that Harihara, the son of Saṅgama, was one of the bravest generals of the Hoysaḷa army; and this supposition would be substantiated by the fact that Dēvappa Hariyappa is called "the strong man of Lakkaṇṇa". Both things, the latter epithet and the above supposition, seem to point to the same person. Anyhow at the present stage of research, we are not able to do anything more than to make a mere suggestion.

* * *

It has been emphasized towards the end of the second lecture that the whole country of Mysore had, after the death

---

[1] *Ep. Carn.*, VII, Sh, 19.

of the last Hoysaḷa King, recognized the authority of Harihara I, apparently without any exception. Ballāḷa IV seems to have died in 1346, and in the same year Harihara is acknowledged east and west of Mysore. But there is an inscription of the same year which shows that even the feudatory petty kings who served under the Hoysaḷas at once transferred their allegiance to Harihara. This inscription is situated in the Tirtahaḷḷi Taluka and commemorates a grant of land made by the Pāṇḍya Chakravarti, Vīra Kāya. Unfortunately a portion of the king's name is lost, but there cannot remain any doubt about who this Pāṇḍya king was. He evidently belonged to the family of the Pāṇḍyas of Uchchangi. These rulers had been subdued by Ballāḷa II [1], and had from this date onwards remained faithful to their overlords. Now in 1346, when the last representative of the Hoysaḷa family disappears, the Pāṇḍya Chakravartti at once recognizes "the mahāmaṇḍaleśvara, master of the eastern, western and northern oceans, subduer of hostile kings, champion over kings who break their word vīra-Hariyappa-Voḍeyar"[2].

One of the important facts proved in the first lecture was that the city of Vijayanagara was founded by Vīra Ballāḷa III of the Hoysaḷa-vaṁśa. The reasons for accepting this view are the statements of Ferishta and Nuniz, which are wonderfully corroborated by the Hoysaḷa inscriptions.

Nevertheless after a long visit of eight days to the ruins of Vijayanagara and to the city of Ānegondi, I have been forced to modify my opinion.

While reading the account of Ferishta, one clearly sees

---

[1] *Ep. Carn.*, XI, Hk, 56.
[2] *Ep. Carn.*, VIII, Tl, 154.

that Ballāḷa III built 'the strong city' which he called Vijayanagara, as a part of a great scheme devised at the assembly of Tiruvaṇṇāmalai in order "to secure the forts of his own country"[1]. Now after the study of the topography and the ruins of Vijayanagara, it is evident that the only fortifications to the north of Vijayanagara are the fortifications crowning all the hills north of the Tuṅgabhadrā in the surroundings of Ānegondi. South of the Tuṅgabhadrā there are no other fortifications or walls but the seven enclosures that run more or less parallel east, south and west. But the fortifications of Ānegondi are the only fortifications of Vijayanagara to the north, whence the Muhammadan lords were expected at any moment in the time of the Tiruvaṇṇāmalai assembly.

It is therefore evident that the fortifications built by Ballāḷa III on this occasion are the fortifications of Ānegondi, by which the pass of the Tuṅgabhadrā was made practically impossible for the Mussulman invaders. Accordingly the foundation of Vijayanagara by the Hoysaḷa monarch, spoken of by Ferishta and confirmed by the Portuguese cronicler, means nothing else than the fortification of Ānegondi, perhaps the enlargement of this city and the renaming of it after his son Prince Virūpāksha, as Śrī-Vīra-Vijaya-Virūpākshapura.

That Ānegondi belonged to the Hoysaḷa Empire some architectonical remains of the place evidently declare. Next to the mantapa on the right between the first and the second prākāra of the Ranganathaswami temple at Ānegondi, there is a beautifully carved black pillar with its capital in purely Hoysaḷa style of the flourishing period of Belur and Hale-

---

[1] Ferishta-Briggs, I, p. 427.

bid. Such delicate lace-like carvings were never produced but under the tutelar care of the Hoysaḷa monarchs.

This new opinion of the fortification, enlargement and renaming of the city of Ānegondi by Ballāḷa III is confirmed by several inscriptions of the time of different Vijayanagara Emperors:—

A. *Inscriptions of Harihara I.*

There are two inscriptions that mention the residence of Harihara I: one of the year 1336 gives the city of Vidyānagara [1]; but this is an inscription which according to Mr. Rice is not genuine.

The other inscription of the year 1347 mentions the city of Hastini (Ānegondi) which is said to be "protected by the king Harihara together with his brother" [2]. It is therefore clear that Hastini or Ānegondi was the capital of his kingdom.

There is moreover another inscription of the year 1336-7, but fabricated at a much later period[3], (and with this several other inscriptions which are probably also concocted) that narrates the meeting of Harihara with Vidyāraṇya, after the former had crossed the Tuṅgabhadrā coming from the city of Kuñjarakōṇa (Ānegondi). These inscriptions, though faked in later times, seem nevertheless to transmit to us the ancient tradition that the Empire of Vijayanagara originated at Ānegondi. The Portuguese chronicler Nuniz in his account of the city of Negundin (Ānegondi) is another channel through which the same tradition has come to us [4].

---

1 *Ep. Carn.*, X, Bg, 70.
2 *Ep. Carn.*, VIII, Sb, 375.
3 Butterworth, *Nellore Inscriptions*, I, p. 114.
4 Cf. supra, pp. 2-3.

B. *Inscriptions of Bukka I.*

Towards the end of the first lecture it was proved that Hosapaṭṭana, which is given in several inscriptions as the residence of Bukka I, is the same city of Vijayanagara[1]. This name is now satisfactorily explained. Bukka I, after "having conquered the whole world", says one of his inscriptions, "built a splendid city called the city of victory"[2]. Since it was supposed that Vijayanagara was founded by Ballāḷa III, this phrase was not easily understood. "The meaning of this phrase", we wrote above, "is not precisely that Bukka built a new city but that he so enlarged and beautified the old one that he may be said in some way to have built a new capital"[3]. Now nevertheless the meaning is obvious. Bukka is the real founder of Vijayanagara, south of the Tuṅgabhadrā[4]. And this is the reason why in many of his inscriptions Vijayanagara is called Hosapaṭṭana[5], the new city, comparing it with the old town of Ānegondi. This explains the fact that in the inscription which records the building of Vijayanagara by Bukka, the description of the new town is given in detail.

C. *Inscriptions of Harihara II.*

An inscription of 1395, that has been mentioned above, calls Harihara II, "the supreme lord of the royal city Hastināpura - Vijayanagara"[6]. This shows that the old city of Ānegondi and the new city of Vijayanagara were not two

1 Cf. supra, pp. 56-57.
2 *Ep. Carn.*, V, Cn, 256.
3 Supra, p. 58.
4 Such is Couto's statement. Cf. Sewell, p. 222.
5 Cf. supra, p. 56.
6 *Ep. Carn.*, VIII, Sb, 103.

cities, but only one, the portion south of the Tuṅgabhadrā being an extension of the northern portion, which is accordingly mentioned the first.

This preference of Ānegondi to Vijayanagara is manifest in another inscription of Harihara II, of the year 1399. This epigraph states that Harihara II, "was in the residence of Vijayanagari in the Hastināvati fort"[1]. This phrase shows first, that Hastināvati was more important than Vijayanagara; second that the importance of Hastināvati or Anegondi lay in the fact that it was a fort, in fact the only fort of Vijayanagara, at least to the north. This importance of the fort of Ānegondi for the royal "residence of Vijayanagari" clearly indicates that that fort was the beginning of Vijayanagara itself and consequently it implicitly confirms the belief in the fortification of Ānegondi by Ballāḷa III.

D. *Inscriptions of Dēva Rāya II.*

In the year 1432 Dēva Rāya II is said to be "in the residence of Hampe-Hastināvati, which is Vijayanagari"[2]. This statement clearly confirms the view that Vijayanagara was the royal residence at the capital of the Empire (at least the earliest one), which was Hampe-Hastināvati, *viz.* Ānegondi, the one near the Pampa. This is still more evidently seen in another inscription of Dēva Rāya of the year 1420. In this record he is said to be " in the residence of Vidyānagari belonging to Ānegondi-durga, which is Hampe-Hastināvati[3]. " Accordingly the fortress of Vijayanagara, the real stronghold against the northern Mussulmans, was Ānegondi-durga, and that, and no other, must have been the fortress

1 *Ep. Carn.*, VIII, Hl, 71.
2 *Ep. Carn.*, V, Cn, 241.
3 *Ep. Carn.*, VII, Sk, 288.

that was rebuilt, or at least strengthened, when Ballāḷa III decided to fortify the northern frontier of his Empire.

Thus it is evident that the craddle of the Empire of Vijayanagara is Ānegondi, and that the Empire itself was born there in order to defend the south against the Muhammadan invasions. This conclusion is finally corroborated by the rumours current in Vijayanagara about the city of Anegondi, faithfully recorded by Paes in his chronicle: "There is a city built there (on the bank of the river)," says he, "which they call Senagumdym (Śri Ānegondi) and they say that of old it was the capital of the kingdom"[1].

---

[1] Sewell, *The Forgotten Empire*, p. 259.

INDEX

Achyuta Dēva Rāya, 8, 12, 26, 27, 29, 34 n1, 54, 57, 60, 114.

Adil Shahi Capital, 44. *See* Bijapur.

Afghan, 95, 61, 36.

Ahmadnagar, 43.

Ahmudnuggar. *See* Ahmadnagar.

Ahmad Shah Bahmāni, 9.

Aiyangar, Dr. S. Krishnaswami, 14.

Ajarāo, 46, 47.

Aka Hurryhur, 61, 62. *See* Harihara I.

Alaka, 2, 3, 7.

Alija Gangi Dēva daṇṇāyaka, 90.

Alla-ud-din Hassan Shah Gangu Bahmāni, 116.

Alla-ud-din Khilji, 49, 116.

Ananda Kōṇ, 10.

Anant, 74.

Andhra, 118, 119, 120, 122.

Andra, 118.

Andray, 61.

Anebidehalla, 77.

Ānegondi, 1, 2, 22, 26, 36, 48, 50, 51, 52, 53, 54, 63, 127, 128, 129, 130, 131, 132.

Ānegondi-durga, 51, 131.

Aṅga, 118, 120.

Araga, 17, 18, 100.

Āralahāḷ Mārapa, 109.

Āravīdu Dynasty, 62, 63.

Aryiappa Uḍaiyar, 93, 99, 111.

Arulahāl Māragauḍa, 109.

Aruṇasamudra, 65.

Badami, 68.

Bagiyūr, 76,

Bahmāni Dynasty of Gulbarga, 10.

Bahmāni Sultanates, 43.

Baicheya-daṇṇāyaka-chamūpa, 124.

Balgaṛchche, 76.

Ballāḷa I, 79, 80.

Ballāḷa II, 76, 83, 84, 89, 96, 122.

Ballāḷa III, 42, 44, 46, 48, 49, 55, 58, 64, 66, 67, 68, 69, 77, 87, 89, 90, 92, 93,

94, 95, 97, 99, 100, 104, 105, 109, 110, 115, 116, 118, 123, 124, 125, 126, 127, 128, 130, 131, 132.
Ballāḷa IV, 91, 99, 103, 105, 106, 109, 110, 111, 112, 113, 127.
Ballappadaṇṇāyaka, 104, 105, 124.
Bāllapa Mantri, 98.
Banavase. *See* Banavasi.
Banavasi, 100.
Banavasi Twelve Thousand, 14, 18.
Bangalore, 22, 23, 104.
Bangalore District, 106, 108, 109.
Bangalore Taluka, 99, 103, 108.
Barakūra-Rājya, 103,.
Bārakūru, 67.
Beeja, 42, 44.
Beejanuggar, 42. *See* Vijayanagara.
Beejapoor, 43. *See* Bijapur.
Begūr Hobli, 103.
Belala Rajas, 62.
Beḷgali, 76.
Belur, 69, 116, 117, 128.
Bemmatūra-durga, 91.
Bemmatūra-kallu, 124.
Benares, 15, 18.
Beṭṭarasa, 76.
Bhadra, 70 n6, 77.
Bhārati-Kṛishna-tīrtha, 15, 16, 18, 35 n3, 104.
Bhārati-tīrtha-Śrīpāda. *See* Bhārati-Krishna-tīrtha.
Bhīma Rāja, 124, 125.
Bhōginatha, 98.
Bhuvanēśvara, 10.
Bichenegher, 65.
Bīdar, 9.
Bijapur, 43.
Bilal Dew. *See* Ballāḷa III.
Billapa-daṇṇāyaka, 105. *See* Ballapa-daṇṇāyaka.
Bisnaga. *See* Vijayanagara.
Bitragunta, 63, 94, 95, 98, 102, 115, 118.
Bodayya Rāja, 53.
Bodha Mahādēva, 54, 108.
Bombay, 13 n3.
Booka. *See* Bukka I.
Brahma, 17.
Brihaspati, 101, 116.
Buchanan, Francis, 61.
Bucarão, 46, 47, 48.
Bukka, 54, 74 n8, 75 n.
Bukka I, 9, 15, 16, 18, 19, 20, 29, 30, 34, 46, 47, 48, 50, 54, 55, 56, 57, 58, 59, 61, 62, 63, 64, 68 n2, 70, 74, 77, 79, 80, 93, 94, 96, 97, 98, 99, 100, 101, 106, 107, 108, 109, 111, 112, 113, 114,

115, 116, 117, 118, 119, 120, 130.
Bukka II, 21, 22, 47, 76, 83, 84, 89, 96, 122, 127.
Burnell, 32.
Butterworth, 4, 14 n8.
Canara, 62,
Canarese, 63.
Carnatic, 42, 62, 95.
Chalukyas, 53.
Chamarāja, 68.
Chandragupti. *See* Chandragutti.
Chandragutti, 14, 77, 100, 102.
Chauda, 10.
Chennakēśavanātha, 117.
Chēra, 73.
Chikka Ariyaṇṇa, 109.
Chikka Rāya, 17, 18, 19.
Chitaldroog, 20, 22, 23, 25, 26, 27, 28, 32, 33, 90, 91.
Chitaldroog Taluka, 34, 44, 124.
Chitaldroog District, 106, 107.
Chōḷas, 73, 105.
Coorg, 74 n4.
Couto, 59.
Cruickshank Road, 13 n3.
Cuddapah District, 94.
Dādi Sōmaya Daṇṇāyaka, 90, 91, 92, 93, 97.
Dāma-daṇḍēśa, 76.
Dāma-Rāya, 75.
Dātiya-Somaiya-daṇṇāyakkar. *See* Dādi Sōmaya Daṇṇāyaka.
Deccan, 43, 95.
Delhi, 36, 37, 41, 42, 49, 50, 68, 95, 103, 115.
Delly, 42. *See* Delhi.
Deorão, 1, 39, 40, 46, 48.
Dēvappa Hariyappa, 127.
Dēvarasa, 76.
Dēva Rāya I, 22, 23.
Dēva Rāya II, 24, 31, 50 51, 56, 113, 115, 131.
Dharmakarta, 53.
Dhorasamudra, 68 n2.
Dilli, 42. *See* Delhi.
D'jemal-addin Mohammed, 68 n3.
Dōrasamudra, 44, 49, 65, 66, 67, 100, 106, 123.
Durga, 54, 108.
Dvarāvati, 57.
Dvārāvatipura, 115.
Elliot, Sir Walter, 56, 57.
Emmatūra-durga, 90.
Enybiquymelly, 38.
Eṛeyanga, 75.
Fergusson, 52.
Ferishta, 10, 42, 43, 44, 45, 49, 89, 123, 125, 127.
Fleet, Dr. J. F., 32, 50.

Gadag, 53.
Gajapati, 73.
Gālāmbikā, 69.
Gandikotā, 53.
Ganga Maṇḍala, 126.
Gaunda Daṇḍanātha, 120.
Gaurambika, 69.
Ghiyath-ud-din, 69.
Gōmanta-Saila, 100.
Gopinatha Rao, 17, 52, 64.
Gunda Daṇḍanātha, 117, 121.
Guru, 101.
Gutti, 101.
Haḍavaḷike- nāḍ, 126.
Hadināḍ, 98.
Haive, 100, 103.
Hakka, 47.
Halebid, 128, 129.
Hampi, 10, 13, 16, 18, 25, 48, 50, 52, 58.
Hampe-Hastināvati, 23, 25, 26, 27, 28, 41, 53, 57, 93, 110, 131.
Hampe-Voḍeyar, 28, 110.
Hariab, 68 n3.
Harihara I, 2, 3, 4, 6, 8, 10, 12, 14, 15, 16, 17, 18, 19, 29, 34, 46, 48, 50, 51, 52, 54, 58, 59, 60, 61, 62, 63, 64, 65, 67, 68, 68 n2&3, 69, 76, 77, 77 n4, 90, 91, 92, 93, 94, 95, 96, 97, 98, 99, 100, 101, 102, 104, 105, 106, 110, 111, 113, 114, 115, 118, 125 n1, 126, 127, 129.
Harihara II, 15, 16, 17, 20, 21, 30, 31, 45, 47, 50, 105. 109, 112, 113, 114, 115, 116, 117, 120, 121, 131.
Harihara-Mahārāya, 12, 34. *See* Harihara I.
Harihara Rāya I, 12. *See* Harihara, I.
Hariya Hariyappa-oḍeyar, 105. *See* Harihara I.
Hariyapoḍeyar, 104. *See* Harihara I.
Hassan, 11, 20, 21, 22, 23, 25, 26, 27, 32, 33, 108.
Hastinati, 21. *See* Hastināvati.
Hastināvati, 19, 20, 21, 24, 25, 27, 28, 50, 53, 55, 95, 131.
Hastināpura, 55.
Hastināpura Vijayanagara, 21, 50, 130.
Hastini, 19, 50, 102, 129.
Hēmakūta, 59.
Heras, S. J., Rev. H., 13 n3.
Himālayas, 72.
Honavar, 68, 102.
Hosabeṭṭa, 58, 66.
Hosahaḷḷi, 74.
Hosanāḍ, 66.

Hosa-Hampeya-Paṭṭaṇa, 57, 58, 60.
Hosapaṭṭaṇa, 19, 55, 56, 57, 59, 60, 106, 130.
Hoskote Taluka, 67, 106.
Hospet, 59, 60.
Hoysaḷa (style, army, inscriptions, etc.), 44, 67, 74, 99, 108, 126, 127, 128, 129.
Hoysaḷa Ballāḷas, 63.
Hoysaḷa Ballāḷa Mahārāja, 109.
Hoysaḷa Empire, 43 n, 48, 49, 56, 77, 77 n4, 100, 102, 106, 115, 116, 128.
Hoysaḷa Emperor, 90, 109, 110, 111, 113, 114, 122.
Hoysaḷa-nāḍ, 115.
Hoysaḷānvaya, 89.
Hoysaḷas, 48, 53, 75, 77 n6, 89, 97, 114, 118, 118 n1, 121, 127.
Hoysaḷa-vaṁśa (dynasty or family), 65, 78, 88, 93, 104, 110, 118, 127.
Hoysaḷa Yādava Chakravarti, 84.
Hoysana Country Kings, 56, 57, 105, 106, 116, 117.
Hukkanā Oḍeyar, 75 n.
Hyderabad Dynasty, 113.
Ibn Batuta, 68, 102.
Ibrahim Adil Shah, 44.
Ikeri Nāyaks, 10.
Indra, 95.
Irā-Sārasavti, 3.
Jainas, 107.
Jamall-ud-din Muhammad, 68 n3.
Janamējaya, 55.
Janārdan, 74.
Jangu, 11.
Jinji, 10.
Jinji Taluka, 107.
Kadam, 65.
Kādamba, 100.
Kadamba Dynasty, 100.
Kadūr, 19, 20, 21, 22, 23, 24, 25, 26, 27, 28, 32, 77 n6.
Kadūr District, 33, 104, 107, 109.
Kākare-nāḍ, 117.
Kākatīya Dynasty or family, 49, 61, 63, 95.
Kākatīya Rāja, 62, 64.
Kalachurris, 53.
Kālamēgha, 24.
Kalasa, 77.
Kali-nadiyama-nāḍ Four Thousand, 117.
Kalingas, 118, 119, 120, 121, 122.
Kallasa, 77.
Kāma Hoysaḷa, 78.
Kāmāji, 69.
Kāmākshi, 69.

Kāmambika, 69.
Kampa, 64, 94, 95, 97, 100, 102.
Kampana or Kumpaṇṇa, 96, 101, 108, 117.
Kampaṇṇoḍeyar, 94, 96, 97, 104.
Kamparāja, 98.
Kancanhalli Taluka, 109.
Kanarese Country, 121.
Kapa Mahārāja, 53.
Karnaṭaka, 73, 76, 89, 106, 111, 113.
Karnaṭaka-dēśa, 73.
Kārtāvirya, 72.
Kaṭhōra-Hara, 124, 125.
Kāvēri, 73, 107.
Kēladi, 54.
Kēladi Arāsa Vaṁśāvaḷi, 10.
Kella-naḍu, 107.
Kēralas, 120.
Kaśava, 75, 116, 117.
Kēśava-chamunātha, 75.
Kēśavadanḍaṇātha, 76, 89.
Kēśirāja, 76, 78, 88, 91.
Khaṇinga, 122.
Kinkunda-naḍu, 107.
Kistna. *See* Kṛishṇa.
Kōdavalūru, 94, 97.
Kolar, 4, 19, 21, 22, 23, 27, 32.
Kolar District, 2, 26, 97, 104.
Konkana, 55, 103.
Kratupura, 53.
Kṛishṇa, 57, 62, 114.
Kṛishṇa Dēva Rāya, 8, 25, 26, 29, 59, 60, 114.
Krishnamacharlu, 14.
Krishna Naig. *See* Kṛishṇa Nāyaka.
Kṛishṇa Nāyaka, 66, 95, 123.
Kṛishṇa Rāya, 54, 60.
Kriyā Śakti, 100.
Kubēra, 2, 3.
Kuḍuvaḷḷi, 34.
Kumāra Kampaṇṇa. 98, 107, 108, 115, 116.
Kumāra Sōvaṇṇoḍeyar, 104.
Kuñjarakōṇa, 19, 29, 50.
Kuñjarakōṇapuri, 29, 50, 51.
Kuntala, 56.
Kuntala-dēśa, 57.
Kuruba, 10, 62.
Kutakas, 120.
Lākkaṇṇa, 126.
Lakshmi, 59.
Lingaṇṇa Nāyaka, 109.
Lisbon, 36.
Luddur Dew, 95. *See* Rudra Dēva.
Maabir, 44.
Mackenzie Collection, 62.
Mādhava, 10, 11, 14, 16, 35 n3, 76, 100, 101.
Mādhavācharya, 15.
Mādhava Rāya, 124.

Mādhava Vidyāraṇya, 16,17, 32, 97.
Madavīyā Dhātuvṛiṭṭi, 97.
Madhura, 73. *See* Madura.
Madura, 49,69,74,92,103,116.
Mayili Nāyaka, 109-110.
Māgāmbikā, 74.
Mahābhārata, 52.
Mahāsen, 3, 6.
Malāmbika, 69.
Malidēva-daṇḍādhipati, 75.
Male-rājya, 100.
Mallachamūpa, 76.
Mallapa, 76.
Mallikārjuna, 24, 114.
Mallik Kafur, 42, 49.
Mallik Naib, 38, 39.
Malur Taluka, 96, 104.
Manāmbika, 69.
Manubhūsha, 73, 74.
Māra, 94.
Māra-Dēva, 109.
Mārapa, 14, 34, 77, 94, 99, 100, 101.
Mārapa Voḍeyar, 18.
Mārapoḍeyar, 104.
Marappa, 93-94.
Māyāmbika, 74.
Mēgāmbika, 74.
Mēlepāḷu, 34.
Meliquy Niby, 38, 40.
Mēru, 107.
Milinebiquy, 39.
Mudda, 94.
Muddana, 94.
Muddapa, 94, 101.
Muddapoḍeyar, 104.
Mudra Chiddi Sāyanna Oḍayalu, 97.
Mughal Emperor, 113.
Muhammadabad, 9.
Muhammad bin Tuglak, 116.
Muhammad Tuglak, 11, 36, 41, 42, 49.
Mukunda, 57.
Mysore, 21, 26, 32, 63, 64, 90, 97, 103, 104, 105, 107, 126, 127.
Nagalapur, 60.
Nagallapor, 59.
Nagundy, 37, 39. *See* Ānegondi.
Nagumdym, 1, 2, 5, 6, 36.
Nallūr, 76.
Nanda Mahārāja, 52.
Nārada, 117.
Nāraṇa Dēva Voḍeyar, 109.
Narasiṁha, 25, 31.
Narasiṁha (Hoysaḷa), 76.
Narasiṁha I, 82, 83.
Narasiṁha II, 85.
Narasiṁha III, 86.
Narasa Rāya, 54.
Narasimhachar, 30.
Navakhaṇḍa, 52.
Nāyaks of Tarikeri, 9.

Negundin, 129. *See* Anegondi.
Nellore, 3, 4, 19, 27, 32, 98.
Nellore District, 2, 14 n8, 94, 95, 97.
Nijagali Kataka Rāya, 55.
Nikitin, 65.
Nizam, 113.
Noḷamba Vīra, 55.
Noḷamba Dynasty, 55.
North Kanara, 100.
Nuniz (Fernão), 1, 2, 4, 5 n1, 8, 35, 36, 40, 41, 42, 43 n, 45, 46, 47, 48, 59, 60, 127, 129.
Ootacamund, 13.
Paes, 60, 132.
Pampa, 2, 12, 52, 131.
Pampādēvi, 6, 48.
Pampāpati, 53.
Paṇḍya, 73.
Paṇḍya Chakravarti, 127.
Paṇḍya Dēva, 77.
Paṇḍyas, 77, 105.
Paṇḍyas of Uchchangi, 127.
Parīkshit, 55.
Pariya-ghaṭṭa, 117.
Panugoṇḍe, 90. *See* Penukoṇḍa
Penukoṇḍa, 43 n, 90.
Poddarāsa, 97.
Portuguese, 35, 59, 129.
Poysaḷa, 75, 88.
Poysaḷa Śrī-Vīra Vallāḷa Dēva, 92. *See* Ballāla III.
Poysaḷa-vaṁśa. *See* Hoysaḷa-vaṁśa.
Pratāpa Rudra, 63.
Prithuvi-gāmunda, 70.
Purandara, 2, 7.
Pureoyre Deorão, 46, 47, 48.
Raghunāthasvami Temple, 128.
Rājakālanirṇaya, 9, 64.
Ramappa Varmika, 61.
Rāma II, 28, 114.
Rāmchandra Bhārati, 34, 86.
Ramadaṇḍādhipa, 75.
Rāmanatha, 86, 87.
Ramēśvara, 71.
Ramēśvaram, 73.
Ranga III, 28.
Rangachari, V., 63.
Rāya Vamśāvaḷi, 52, 53.
Reddi, 74 n8.
Rice (Lewis), 4, 29, 30, 35 n2, 51, 55, 56, 63, 64, 65, 129.
Rudra, 64.
Rudra Dēva, 95.
Russian, 64.
Sadāśiva Rāya, 8, 27, 28, 29, 34 n1, 54, 57, 109.
Śaiva, 15.
Śaivagamasāra, 101.
Śakra, 100.
Saḷa, 78, 88, 89, 117.

Saṁgama, 46. *See* Saṅgama (I).
Samgama Rāja. *See* Saṅgama II.
Saṅgama Dynasty, 63, 65, 97.
Saṅgama (I), 69, 70, 71, 73, 74, 75 n, 76, 77, 78, 89, 93, 99, 100, 101, 121, 126.
Sangama. *See* Saṅgama (I).
Sangama (village) 70.
Saṅgama II, 95, 96, 98, 115, 118.
Saṅgama Nripēndra. *See* Saṅgama (I).
Saṅgamēśa, 2, 5, 70, 71. *See* Saṅgama (I).
Saṅgamēśvara, 70. *See* Saṅgama I.
Sangamēśvara (town), 77.
Sangamēśvarat, 70. *See* Saṅgama I.
Śanka, 93, 103.
Śankapārya, 103.
Sānta, 124.
Śārada, 69, 94.
Śaśakapura, 88.
Śasimauli, 72.
Sastri, Hirananda, 13 n3.
Sastri, Krishna H., 14, 68 n2, 96, 110.
Satalige-nāḍu, 107.
Sayanna Oḍayalu. *See* Sayanna.
Sayanna, 11, 97, 98.
Senagumdym. *See* Ānegondi.
Seringapatam, 73.
Seringapatam Taluka, 70.
Sēsha, 3.
Sewell, 2 n1, 9, 14, 40, 43 n, 46, 47, 51, 52, 62, 65, 99.
Shikarpur Taluka, 55.
Shimoga, 19, 20, 21, 22, 23, 25, 26, 27, 28, 32, 33.
Shimoga District, 108.
Siddaya, 109.
Sigala-nāḍ, 109.
Siṁha-Dēva, 122.
Siṁhana, 85.
Siṁha-Raghunātha, 124.
Singe-daṇṇāyakar. *See* Singeya-daṇṇāyaka.
Singeya-daṇṇāyaka, 27, 67, 91, 92, 124.
Śiva, 3, 17, 72, 125.
Śivappa Nāyaka of Ikeri, 12.
Smith, Vincent, 63, 112.
Śōmappa, 96, 97.
Sōmappa Daṇṇāyaka, 97, 107, 109,
Sōmayya Daṇṇāyaka, 90, 91.
Sōmarasa, 91.
Sōmēśvara, 85, 86.

Sōmeya Daṇṇāyaka, *See* Sōmayya Daṇṇāyaka
Sorab, 101.
Sorab Taluka, 77, 99, 108.
Sosavur, 77 n6, 117, 118.
South Arkot District, 107, 108.
Śravana Belgola, 107.
Śrīdhara-daṇḍanātha, 75.
Śringeri Jagir, 12.
Śringeri, 15, 16, 18, 33, 34, 35, 77, 101, 104, 105, 107.
Śrīpāda, 15. *See* Vydyātirtha Śrīpāda.
Śrīrangapaṭṭaṇa, 73.
Srī-Toragal, 53.
Srī Vīra Vijaya Virūpākshapura, 45, 48, 50, 55, 57, 65, 66, 90, 92.
St. Xavier's College, 13 n3.
Suryanarain Row, 11, 12, 13, 14, 52, 53, 63, 75 n.
Sutrāman, 115,
Talikota, 12.
Talirūr, 76.
Tamil, 104.
Tanan, 92.
Tancha, 73.
Tanjore, 73.
Tārīk-i-Firoz Shāhi, 44.
Tauluvas, 120.
Tazrat-ul-Mulūk, 9.
Tēkal, 96.
Telinga, 61, 62, 63.
Telingana, 49.
Telugu, 62, 63, 64, 74 n8, 94, 98, 103, 118, 119, 120.
Telugus, 121, 122.
Tepaṇṇa-Voḍeyar, 117.
Teppada-Nāgaṇṇa-Voḍeyar, 117.
Tirthahaḷḷi Taluka, 127.
Tirukkōyilur Taluka, 108.
Tirumala Rāya, 28.
Tiruvaṇṇāmalai, 49, 66, 68 n2, 99, 123, 125, 128.
Toombudra, 61. *See* Tuṅgabhadrā.
Tryāmbaka, 101.
Tuluva, 61.
Tumkūr, 19, 20, 21, 22, 23, 24, 25, 26, 27, 28, 32.
Tumkūr District, 121.
Tuṅga, 70 n6. *See* Tuṅgabhadrā.
Tuṅgabhadrā, 2, 3, 4, 5, 51, 52, 55, 56, 59, 61, 70, 70 n6, 88, 128, 129, 131.
Turushka, 73, 105, 120.
Vaishnavas, 107.
Vajiyaṇṇa, 106.
Vallāḷa, 92. *See* Ballāḷa I.
Vallaḷa Dēvar 67. *See* Ballāḷa III.
Vallapa, 92, 93.

Vanavāse Twelve Thousand, 100. See Banavasi Twelve Thousand.
Vanuigahalli, 109.
Vārānasi, 15. See Benares.
Vartūr Hobli, 104.
Vasadhāre-sīme, 34.
Velanagara, 116.
Velapura, 116, 117.
Veṅkaṭa II, 28.
Veṅkaṭa IV, 28, 114.
Veṅkaṭadri, 54.
Venkagga, 74 n9.
Venugopaul Chetty, 74 n8.
Videyanuggur, 62.
Videyarannea, 62.
Vidyā, 2, 3, 7, 19. See Vydyānagara.
Vidyānagar. See Vidyānagara.
Vidyānagara, 11, 12, 19, 22, 23, 25, 27, 28, 33, 57, 62, 129.
Vidyānagari. See Vidyānagara.
Vidyāraṇya, 2, 3, 6, 7, 9, 10, 11, 12, 13, 14, 15, 16, 18, 19, 31, 32, 33, 34, 35, 40, 53, 62, 101, 129.
Vidyāraṇyapura, 12, 15.
Vidyāśaṅkara, 35.
Vidyātīrtha, 16, 35.
Vidyatīrtha Śrīpāda, 18, 105.
Vijaya, 20, 22, 23, 42, 44, 45, 57. See Vijayanagara.
Vijayadhwaja, 52.
Vijayanagar. See Vijayanagara.
Vijayanagara, 1, 3, 5, 9, 10, 11, 13, 14, 15, 16, 17, 18, 19, 20, 21, 22, 23, 24, 25, 26, 27, 28, 29, 30, 31, 32, 33, 34, 35, 36, 37, 39, 40, 41, 42, 43, 44, 47, 48, 49, 50, 51, 53, 54, 55, 56, 57, 58, 60, 61, 62, 63, 64, 65, 67, 68, 74 n8, 75, 77, 78, 92, 93, 95, 96, 99, 102, 107, 108, 109, 112, 113, 114, 115, 118, 120, 121, 122, 125, 127, 128, 129, 130, 131, 132.
Vijayanagari. See Vijayanagara.
Vijaya Rayal, 52.
Vijaya Vīra, 23.
Vikramāsiṁhapura, 64.
Vinayāditya, 56, 75, 79, 89.
Vīra Kāya, 127.
Vīra Narasiṁha, 25.
Vīra Vijaya, 22, 31.
Virūpāksha, 2, 4, 5, 12, 15, 25, 31, 45, 52, 55, 59, 114.
Virūpāksha Ballāḷa Dēva, 44, 110.
Virūpāksha-Dēva, 3, 10 n6.

Virūpākshapāda, 67.
Virūpākshapaṭṭaṇa, 66, 67.
Virūpākshapura, 95. *See* Vijayanagara.
Virupaṇṇa, 101.
Vīra Virupa Rāya, 101.
Visaya Nagar, 59.
Vishṇu, 17, 57, 71, 116.
Vishṇuvardhana Bitti Dēva Rāya, 76, 80, 81, 82, 100, 107, 115, 116, 117, 118, 122.
Vriddhachalam Taluka, 108.
Vydyātīrtha, 15.
Warangal, 49, 61, 62, 63, 64, 66, 95, 123.
Warankal. *See* Warangal.
Western Ghats, 117.
Wilks, Col. Mark, 61, 62.
Wilson, H. H. 62, 74 n1.
Wurungole. *See* Warangal.
Yādava, 75, 77, 78, 79, 80, 82, 84, 85, 88.
Yādava Chakravarti, 82, 84, 85, 86, 87.
Yādava-kula, vaṁśa or race, 70, 71, 75, 79, 80, 82, 83, 84, 85, 86, 87, 88, 89, 91.
Yādu, 70, 74, 78, 83, 88, 115.
Yadu-kula or -vaṁśa, 78, 80, 81.
Yādava Rāja, 80, 86.
Yādava Ṛāya, 85.
Yādavas, 81, 93.
Yādavas of Devgiri, 75 n.
Yādus, 80.
Yavana, 120.
Ziā-ud-din Barni, 44.